SNOWBALL INVESTING

Wealth That Won't Retire When You Do

Pat Peoples Smith

Apples of Gold Press

Snowball Investing: Wealth That Won't Retire When You Do
Copyright ©2018 by Pat Peoples Smith. All rights reserved.
Apples of Gold Press
Norcross, Georgia

www.snowball-investing.com
Email: SnowballInvestingToday@gmail.com
Follow the Author's Facebook page, *Snowball Investing.*

ISBN 978-0-9600785-0-9

Cover Design and Book Format: Michele Pollock Dalton, www.digitaldaisy.net
Editor: Jo Hunt
Stock Photo Credits: © neyro2008 / www.123rf.com; ©Shutterstock
Printed and bound in the United States of America
First printing December 2018
1 2 3 4 5 6 7 8 9 10

"He who gathers money little by little makes it grow."

PROVERBS 13:11 (NIV)

Contents

· FOREWORD ·

Snowball Investing is a godsend. Having served in the insurance, investment, and wealth management industries for 20+ years, I have sat across the table from clients whose finances were melting away due to insufficient or misguided financial planning. The sudden onset of a health crisis further exasperates a situation such as this, leaving one overwhelmed and with very few options. Even those of us in the financial services world are not exempt from hiccups in life. I know firsthand.

In 2014, I was stricken with a massive stroke. Overnight, I needed round-the-clock care, intensive occupational, physical, and speech therapy services, and a mound of money to shovel at the mounting hospital and home care costs. Without the principles outlined in *Snowball Investing*, my family's finances would have totally melted away.

I've known Pat Peoples Smith since 2005 when my wife became a distributor with Reliv International, Inc. Pat was also a Reliv distributor, and as we became acquainted, I began to admire her wisdom, tremendous sense of humor, and genuine love for people. Pat's experience as an occupational therapist molded her ability to have empathy and offer solutions for people struggling with disabilities. When she told me about her book, I was excited to read it, and now highly recommend it as a *must-read*.

As a financial advisor, I learned that most people, whether wealthy with high incomes and substantial assets, or on the other end of the spectrum, have a problem with the way they think about money. That, ultimately, affects how they spend it, save it, and invest it (or choose *not* to do any of the three responsibly). As a result, money becomes a major source of stress, causing health problems, family dysfunction, and overall unhappiness.

Finances are a critical issue for all families. It's not just about how much you have, but, more importantly, how you **think** about what you have. "For as he thinketh in his heart, so is he" (Proverbs 23:7 KJV). Pat's book is very much about teaching you how to face the truth about your situation, view the correct purpose of money, and replace crippling spending habits with those that will help you reach your long-term retirement goals.

Through powerful testimonies, including her own journey from indebtedness to debt-free world, Pat captures the essence of a much-needed paradigm shift from discontentment (which leads to wasteful spending) to a contented and satisfying lifestyle based upon the principle of stewardship. Using an array of analogies, especially those associated with snow and other precipitous acts, Pat outlines how you can spot everyday money-wasting habits that originate in your thoughts, leading to financial ruin and a poor quality of life. She sounds the urgent cry to face potential end-of-life health care costs and their overwhelming impact on an unprepared household. Changing your habits regarding how you think about and handle money *before* a crisis hits will enable you to reach your full financial potential, and not just have the minimum needed.

Replacing debt payments with asset-protecting, saving and investing strategies is a key concept. If you are paying credit card companies, making car payments, repaying student loans, paying a mortgage, or buying the wrong life insurance for your family's long-term needs, you *aren't* "Snowball Investing"; you are making those financial institutions wealthy, not becoming wealthy yourself. Learn how to think about money correctly and develop a Snowball Investing strategy now for yourself and the good of your family.

No matter where you are in your financial journey (or even if you don't know where to take the first step), Pat's simple approach for people in all age and socioeconomic groups, can help you draft a financial blueprint that will continue to build wealth long after you decide to retire from employment or from being a business owner. Developing a plan is crucial, but not any old plan will do. Pat graciously exposes the holes and missing pieces that existed in her own financial blueprint and the events that precipitated her "about-face" reality turn.

While she has a love for numbers, Pat adamantly affirms that she has no specialized financial training. She demonstrates a teachable heart that is eager to learn about the whole "ball of wax" in terms of financial planning. In *Snowball Investing*, she freely shares all with which she has been enlightened. She endeavors to build a sturdy financial "stool" with all the necessary "legs" so it won't wobble; one that will succeed under all circumstances — market fluctuations, stock or real estate market downturns, premature death, and, in my case, disability and unexpected long-term care needs. She invites you to build your own stool.

No one knows how long they will live; our days are numbered by the Lord (Job 14:5). Pat's wealth-building journey that began in the "red," entered the "black" after perseverance and sacrifice, and continues to snowball today. She beckons you to join her on the slopes. Take your first step and she'll show you how to kill the number one enemy of all budgets, find your financial flakes (even beneath the mud), and start the ball rolling towards a fruitful financial picture. And who knows, you may even gain unimaginable wealth that is out of this world!

I recall the *100-Man Story*, often told in the financial arena Take any group of 100 people at age 25, follow them for 40 years to retirement age, and you will find the following: only one will be wealthy and four will be financially secure; five will still be working, not because they want to, but because they have to; 36 will be dead; the remaining 54 will be dead broke and depending on Social Security, friends, family or charity for their sustenance. What a grim picture that plays itself out every day in America: 5% successful and 95% unsuccessful.

It's been over four years since my life-altering event. I was blessed to work for over 10 years as Director of Investments and Wealth Management with Allen and Furr Insurance Agency. I sold my financial services company and relinquished my securities and exchange licenses. Through a series of twists and turns, I made the decision to move into an assisted-living facility. The fruit of my planning over the years allowed me to select a very nice facility. I am thankful for Pat's *Snowball Investing* principles, which are comparable to a three-legged financial "stool." Because I had all three legs in place, my financial world did not collapse; not even under the weight of a $333,000 health-related expense tab that began only four short years ago and *continues* to run. One of those three legs *alone* has covered the cost *in its entirety*, leaving the remaining two unscathed. What's been my total out-of-pocket cost? $20,000. I can't wait for you to discover the secret to having a balanced stool, as well as life-altering riches beyond your control.

Pat's book is a gift to America, and couldn't have been written at a more crucial time. *Snowball Investing* shines the light on the problem. You decide how soon you want to grab a shovel and start building. And while you're at it, invite someone you love to grab a shovel too!

> Mark Selman
> Founder, Selman Financial Services
> Director of Investments and Wealth Management,
> Allen and Furr Insurance Agency (retired)

· PREFACE ·

Hurry up and write it!" That was the plea from a colleague as we shared "family crisis" stories across adjacent cubicles well over a decade ago. Laura had moved her mother-in-law into her home due to declining health, and the fringes of her mother-in-law's financial stability were beginning to unravel. (Laura would later share that before her passing, the sum of Mom's health costs surpassed the $1 million mark.) While I listened with sympathetic ear, the depths of her dilemma did not hit home, until they hit home.

My parents were married for 52 years. I still remember their 50th anniversary celebration in 1999 as being a grand affair. Scores of family members and friends traveled from near and far on a cold December evening to extend well-wishes. Mom's priceless smile in her stunning red sequin gown and Dad's debonair moves whisking Mom in his arms for a two-minute waltz gave no indication that things would change drastically in less than three years. On April 24, 2002, Mom entered the hospital. On May 1st, exactly one week later, she died; and Dad, nine years her senior, was suddenly left without the love of his life at the age of 88. Despite not having his beloved rib by his side, Dad managed to continue on with life and tend to all of his needs, even working part-time in real estate, while living with my middle brother.

Then the proverbial shoe dropped. Between Thanksgiving and Christmas of 2006, my Dad regressed from walking independently to needing help getting out of a recliner. A little probing revealed a diagnosis of Parkinson's and Dad's concern that the medication might be causing self-injurious thoughts. Learning all of this was analogous to taking a drink from a fire hydrant. It was sudden, it was blasting, and it was emotionally overwhelming.

Life has a way of happening whether we're prepared or not. A phone call from my Aunt Theresa divulged the second shoe-dropping event: Dad had suffered a stroke, affecting his speech and right side, his dominant side. As a therapist, that's *not* what I wanted to hear. Rehab can be tedious, tiresome, and inconclusive. The turn of events began a wave of phone calls, emails, and meetings to execute the agreed-upon plan by my brothers and myself: bring Dad home.

> Life has a way of happening whether we're prepared or not.

No alternative plan entered our minds. After all, both of my maternal grandparents had been cared for at home by their children. So, without question, the Peoples children sprang into action to do what they had always been taught by example: care for parents to the nth degree. Daddy needed care, 24-hour care. A part-time attendant wouldn't do. Occasional drop-ins by well-meaning friends wouldn't be enough. Thankfully, Dad's speech was restored and the paralysis was replaced with generalized weakness, but he could not be left alone for any length of time, and time was costly.

Through prayer and due diligence, my brothers and I organized Dad's needs for round-the-clock assistance. He was blessed to have a compassionate doctor who, in my opinion, extended his rehab stay to allow us to finalize the plans. It also gave Dad such comfort to know that his kids were working tirelessly behind the scenes to make it all happen. For such a complex challenge, and with two of us living out-of-state, we only had a few glitches along the way.

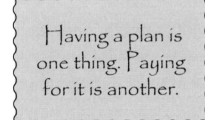

Having a plan is one thing. Paying for it is another.

Having a plan is one thing. Paying for it is another. In our case, the cost was a few dollars shy of $10,000 per month. Every month. In cash. No exceptions. Dad's pension helped to defray less than 1/3 of the cost. The rest came from four kids who loved him dearly. If it meant working extra hours, draining bank accounts, or doing without, meeting his needs was priority.

Each of us siblings had a role to play in Dad's care. One brother took it upon himself to handle a tax situation. The remaining three of us dug in our heels and into our bank accounts to cover the costs. For *each* of us, the in-home care cost was $2200 per month…*every* month…in cash…without exception. In addition, I traveled home once a month during the February-July 2007 period, to cook and freeze a month's worth of meals so Dad wouldn't be eating sodium-laden frozen dinners. Travel costs hovered around $200 in any given month, excluding wear and tear on my car. When Dad paid a scheduled visit to the hospital in August for a *minor* procedure, he caught a staph infection, resulting in a critical 48-hour period, which forced us to have him moved to a skilled facility. That was our introduction to government-assisted care and its litany of limitations and requirements.

For 100 days, our out-of-pocket costs stopped just as quickly as they had begun. From what I can recollect, Dad's Medicare coverage kicked in and paid for 100% of his care. After the 100 days ended, we kids were once again responsible for picking up the difference, including the daily nursing-home bed rate. The basic monthly cost hovered somewhere around $4000. That time was such a blur in my mind, but I do recall shifting from a daughter-to-therapist role and back again on several occasions, arguing for swallow studies, speech therapy services, an upgraded bed to alleviate bed sores (which was unsuccessful), and a specialized chair cushion. The upgrades weren't covered by Medicare. The patient had to incur the costs…the patient's *children* had to incur the costs. So, our Dad's monthly expenses sometimes surpassed the $5000 mark. By the way, all of this happened at a time when Dad's pension funds could not be touched because NONE OF US KIDS WERE ON HIS CHECKING ACCOUNT!

So, what was the total cost? My monthly share of the in-home care expenses: $2200. My travel expenses: $200 per month. My share of Dad's first 100 days in the nursing home was zero. My monthly share of Dad's nursing home stay (while his funds were untouchable) was roughly, $1500. After a miraculous event that released his funds, my share was reduced to $500. My estimated total out-of-pocket costs from the day we brought him home, until the Lord called him home, was $24,600…for 18 months of care. That was my cost *alone*; and I didn't have time to count the cost, I just paid it!

"How did you do it?" you may ask. "How *long* did you do it?" may be another question. Quite frankly, this book would be a two-volume series if I shared all of the twists, turns, and miraculous events that unfolded during this season in our lives. I'll just summarize by saying that none of us kids went bankrupt; none of the bills went unpaid; and we were privileged to have Dad with us until the ripe old age of 94. **If he had had access to Long Term Care insurance, perhaps close to 100% of these costs would have been covered.** (More about this important product later.)

During this period when shoes were dropping on every side, I began to examine my own life. I was single at the time. I had never been married, nor did I have children waiting in the wings to care for me when I wouldn't be able to care for myself. For the most part, income throughout my working career had been steady, but investing had not. Age-wise, I was approaching the half-century mark, and financially speaking, I was not prepared for the second half.

I'm grateful that frugality lay in the recesses of the majority of my decision-making. Having received solid biblical financial teaching early in my adult Christian life, I learned the joy and freedom of not living paycheck-to-paycheck, and to be a generous giver. (Perhaps that's why it was so easy to give towards Dad's needs.) I learned that as God's child, I couldn't manipulate Him to supply every material whim I could conjure up, but I could trust Him to meet my every need, every *real* need.

For over two decades, I tuned into author and financial advisor Larry Burkett's daily radio show, *"Money Matters."* His compassionate and mild-mannered responses to callers' financial struggles reinforced what I had learned at church one eventful morning. (Keep reading; you'll love the story.) Even after Larry transitioned to heaven in 2003, I purposed to follow his teachings with a goal of total debt-free living. That, coincidentally, was the same year that my Dad accelerated my financial goal by paying off my mortgage and car. (As you can see, generosity is in my DNA.) But somehow between Larry's passing in 2003 and my introduction to another radio financial guru in 2006, I made a handful of blunders that wreaked havoc and caused a huge setback in my financial portfolio. It's amazing how a short season without accountability can result in long-term consequences.

Nevertheless, the timing was perfect. A dear friend of mine began sharing some rather bizarre debt-busting and income-saving teaching at her church. They originated from a nationally-known financial advisor who had radio broadcasts across the country. She offered to lend his teaching CDs to me. I wasn't too keen on hearing his voice, but I was intrigued by the successes she shared. So, I borrowed the tapes and designated the last day of the school year as my listening day. That would also be the day I would finally assemble a gas grill that had laid dormant in the box on my deck for almost two years.

I'm a visual, hands-on kind of gal. Give me a screwdriver and I'm a happy camper. That Friday afternoon I couldn't wait to say goodbye to the last student's file, clear off my desk, and head home to a more tangible project. Occupying my mind with biblical financial teaching would be an added bonus. So, the school clothes went off, the work clothes went on, the grill was dragged into the middle of the living room, the standard and Phillips Head were uprooted from the bottom of my toolbox, and the instructions were gently unfolded for the task at hand.

I inserted CD number one and began to sort through the grill pieces. The financial guru wasted no time in unveiling the so-called "stupid tax" that we all tend to pay. My laser focus towards the grill assembly began to drift towards the voice on the CD. That stranger from the radio, the one with the brash voice, was talking to me. Even worse, he was talking *about* me! I listened and I worked. I quickly realized that I needed to take notes, so I grabbed a pad and pen and jotted as fast as my nut-twisting hand could write. I listened and worked and wrote. CD after CD went in and out of my player until I thought it was going to overheat. Why shouldn't it? I was beginning to overheat! The more I listened the more I turned those nuts tighter and tighter to the point of almost stripping them. By the end of the night, every bolt was in place, every nut had been tightened, and I was done! Not with the grill, but with myself! I had no excuses for my dilemma and I was the only one to undo what seemed like a billion blunders! That forged my outlandish attack on debt and my resolve to build the nest egg that I would need in the future.

As I began my personal war on debt, I found myself crossing paths with other unknown soldiers who had reached the same conclusion. They knew that disaster was just around the corner, but they just couldn't see a way to avoid derailment. A familiar statement kept resurfacing: "I can't even save a dollar!" Those words lit a fire and birthed a book in me. "Yes, you *can* save a dollar, yes, you *must* save a dollar, and I'll show you hundreds of ways to do so!" So, that statement, Laura's mother-in-law, my own family crisis, and those annoying CDs set the stage for this book.

"Why another money-saving book?" you might ask. Obviously, the current ones aren't working. Or perhaps they don't speak the language that the common-man can understand and believe he can do. One quick search on any given search engine will produce a list of the wealthiest people in America. We know their names. They're from a relatively short list of categories: entrepreneurs, entertainers, athletes, politicians, and investors, with a few corporate execs sprinkled in the mix. Given five minutes with any one of

them and they will gladly share their wealth-building secret –*Work Hard*. I like the advice that a friend said the owner of an international retail corporation shared with him during an interview in the 80's: "Todd, buy all of our stock that you can afford." Duh! If Todd could have afforded to do that, he wouldn't have been the interviewer, he would have been the interviewee! (Fortunately for him and his family, he found another pathway to building wealth!)

This book is written by an average American *for* average Americans; those who experience shoe-dropping drama day in and day out and don't have a fat bank roll to tackle it; those who can't buy gobs of stock because the mortgage is due and Junior's tuition is right around the corner. This isn't another "get rich quick" book. This is an SOS, 911, eleventh-hour, fourth down and ten, wake-up call, retirement wealth-building manual for screwdriver-wielding maniacs. (I shortened the book's title since I couldn't fit all of it on the cover.) You get the picture.

I had my lightbulb moment. What prompted *you* to pick up this book? Was it a family crisis, your financial statement, a voice on the radio, or just the gut-gnawing reality that math does not lie, the Government is not your mama, and a man with balloons carrying an oversized sweepstakes check is **not** ringing your doorbell? And things are worse than ever. Half of all Americans have nothing saved for retirement. Nothing! This is not the topic discussed around the office water cooler or in social chat rooms.[1] It's embarrassing, it's scary, and it seems absolutely hopeless.

Congratulations, you are way ahead of half of America. The future is tomorrow and you realize that something must be done. It may seem even more impossible if you're a fellow baby boomer who's squandered your hard-earned money on junk that'll end up in the local thrift store before your corpse is cold. Am I being a bit too brash? I'm sorry. This is serious business. We have no time for support-group coddling and patting each other's backs. We have a mess on our hands and we need to get after it, **today!**

Saving a few thousand dollars each year won't build an enormous nest egg, but at least you'll have something in the hen house. If nothing else, it'll allow you and/or your spouse to stay in your home just a little bit

SNOWBALL SNIPPETS

What prompted you to pick up this book?

_____

_____

_____

_____

_____

_____

_____

_____

_____

_____

What are your financial goals for the next 30 days?

1. _____
2. _____
3. _____
4. _____
5. _____

What are your financial goals for the next 60 days?

1. _____
2. _____
3. _____
4. _____
5. _____

longer and be that much less of a burden on your kids, if you're blessed to have any. I'm still on the journey myself. In fact, as we go along chapter by chapter, I'll share my virtual realities with you, the good, the bad, and the ugly. Believe me, there's no pot of gold hidden in my backyard either. Just a few baby snakes, and I've given my husband strict orders to keep them at bay at all costs!

I hope your financial blunders have not exceeded mine. If they have, we'll climb out of our pits of despair together. Better yet, let's build a snowball, a million-dollar snowball. You'll soon discover that thousands can compound into so much more! And if you happen to see my colleague Laura, tell her I finally hurried up.

· ACKNOWLEDGEMENTS ·

It is my pleasure to thank those who contributed to this book.

To my precious parents, Irving and Emma Peoples, for pouring their love into me and blessing me so richly with all the godly and practical wisdom shared in this book. I see your imprint on my life every day; and I miss you each and every day.

To my editor, Jo Hunt, who made many wise queries and suggestions for tidying up my prose. Your patience, laughter, and encouragement are what got me through it all.

To Michele Pollock Dalton, for overseeing all design and formatting elements. You dropped into my life through a Facebook chat. I know you were a gift from God at a time when I was left graphically "high and dry." A wealth of gratitude is extended to you for taking my miniscule idea and transforming it into the perfect cover in a matter of hours.

A wealth of thanks goes to several people who gave the manuscript a thorough read and made thoughtful suggestions: Pastor Roger W.F. Skepple, Sr. (pastor of Berean Bible Baptist Church, Atlanta, GA), Jana Riediger, Mary Anderson, Jerry Black, Katrina Banks, Jeanette Shamis, and Larry Perkins. Special thanks are extended to Mark Selman for schooling me on a valuable missing piece of wealth-building and asset protection. I wish you had been there to manage my portfolio decades ago! I would have been a millionaire by now!

My tenacious snowballing approach would not have ever started without my friend, Sharon Atkins, who graciously shared those invaluable CDs. Sharon, I owe you a debt of gratitude.

To my friend and former colleague, Laura Roadcap. Thank you for your transparency during a family dilemma and your insistence that I "hurry up and write it." It only took me 12 years to complete it, yet your five words kept me reaching for the end product. Now we're both enjoying retirement! Thanks, dear friend.

To Joyce Bray, who championed me every step of the way, suggesting I "just tell stories" when I became stuck in the maze of "facts and figures." Thank you for helping me to unleash a wealth of stories.

To my countless metro Atlanta (and beyond) prayer warriors (you know who you are) and Monday night prayer circle (Holly Berry, Katherine Mott, and Teresa Ulrich), for your continued prayers, love, and encouragement to keep pushing forward. We may never know the total impact of your intercession.

Gratitude must be offered to Tom Fortson for his timely visit to Berean Bible Baptist Church in October 1984, and unfolding the principle of stewardship in such a profound way. Thank you for directing me towards the true Owner of all wealth and my responsibility in dispensing it for His glory.

To my cousin Alma Smith Dixon, the sister I never had. Although no longer with us, thank you for your insistence that we cross the road and meet the neighbors, Jim and Gail Shelton. An eternal gratitude goes to Jim and Gail for fulfilling a divine appointment. My account will never be in the red, although it's covered in red. How ironically blessed I am!

To my amazing husband, Sumner Anthony Smith. Honey, without your love and sacrifice (and willingness to let me hide out in a hotel to tackle those tough chapters), this book would never have made it to print. I love you!

Finally, I am grateful to my Lord and Savior Jesus Christ, who granted me riches that will snowball throughout eternity.

Pat Peoples Smith
Norcross, Georgia, USA
December 2018

· ONE ·

Introduction: *The Sack*

My Mom never sought fanfare. She never dressed in a manner that drew attention to herself. She rarely ever raised her voice to gain attention in a room. But what she did in the bank that day spoke volumes and left an indelible impression on my life.

As early as I can remember, Mom was never comfortable behind a steering wheel. She depended upon Dad and us kids to transport her wherever she wanted to go. My relocation to Atlanta limited my flexibility in traveling home often, but my phone calls with Mom were frequent. One year she began asking when my next visit home would be. With the school year in full swing, I wouldn't be able to break away until summer. She said she had an errand to run. She wanted to open a new account at a new bank, and she wanted me to take her there.

When the school year ended, I made the eight-hour road trip home to Virginia. The next day, after one of Mom's delicious breakfasts, we got dressed, she reached into her closet, grabbed her black purse, and off we headed to the bank. We arrived mid-morning, so the small branch was practically empty. We were immediately greeted by a pleasant bank employee who inquired about the purpose of our visit. Mom expressed a desire to open a new account and make a deposit. The young woman happily obliged and ushered us towards two chairs situated across from her desk. She began outlining the available checking and savings options. It was apparent that Mom fit into the senior citizen age bracket, so the worker included the benefits of a Focus 55 Money Market account, a traditional savings plan, and certificates of deposit in the discussion.

After a thorough presentation, Mom thought for a moment and then announced that she wanted to open accounts for the traditional savings, as well as the Focus 55 option. Assuming she had misunderstood the stipulations of each, and underestimating the contents of her purse, I reclarified that Focus 55 *alone* required a minimum $2500 deposit. She politely nodded and restated her intentions. After the bank worker was sure of Mom's decision, she began to gather the necessary paperwork.

The Indelible Moment

The next moment will forever be etched in my mind. Mom unclasped her purse and pulled out an old wrinkly brown paper sack. Reaching inside, she proceeded to lay payroll check after payroll check on the worker's desk, concluding with a two-inch thick wad of cash. The young woman's facial expression was priceless, as she removed the rubber band that had kept the wad neatly bundled until the appointed time. She thumbed through the bills one by one, shaking her head in disbelief. Pictures of Ben Franklin surfaced over and over. When it was all said and done, the worker couldn't contain herself. She broadcasted to the entire bank that Mom's wrinkly old sack had held over $11,000! Mom didn't like her business being shared, and her frown and raised eyebrow told you so.

Given the fact that this middle-class Black woman was born in the foothills of Tennessee, the second of 14 children, you would probably applaud her for such a remarkable accomplishment. It must have taken her years to scrape together those pennies (or, in this case, "Bennies") for a once-in-a-lifetime event. I would agree with you wholeheartedly, except on one point. This became an event that Mom would repeat time and time again. It almost became an unspoken thriller during trips home when she would request a ride to the bank. No matter the amount, Mom always seemed to have her next deposit tucked inside that wrinkly brown sack. My youngest brother and I were usually the chosen designated drivers. Either we were more accessible to her, or she may have felt we wouldn't blab her business all over town. (Of course, I'm blabbing it right now in a best seller!)

I recall another visit home when Mom and I excused ourselves after dinner, went to our usual meeting place (the blue master bedroom in the rear), and caught up on life's happenings. She shuffled her blue wedged-heel bedroom slippers towards the closet, leaned forward, and grabbed the infamous black purse. She took a seat in her blue crushed velvet wingback chair near the window while I plopped myself on her bed, gearing up for another mathematical moment. This time was different. There were no payroll checks. They had all been cashed, month after month after month. Mom uncovered banded piles from the sack, that little brown sack. Given her past actions, I shouldn't have been surprised, but once again she wowed me. Those precious little bundles totaled $25,000! Guess who was gifted with a fifth of the bundles? (Sometimes it pays to go home! Just kidding.)

Right now, I need to stop and put some things into perspective. By this period in my parents' lives, all but one of my three siblings and I had completed college. My parents' mortgage was minimal. They never had a car note besides the first car Dad bought in the 40's. They were not enamored by the glitz and glamour of billboards and television ads. They lived a modest life. Rumor had it that Mr. Peoples (my Dad) was wealthy. This self-made Arkansas farmer, the youngest of six, who overcame poverty, bought a two-story brick home surrounded by 55 acres of lush farm land. Dad never had a huge bank roll. He strove to make the wisest decisions possible. He was always looking ahead to provide for his family, something that his Dad was never around to do.

We've all had sacks. Most baby boomers have probably carried one to school with a PBJ sandwich and apple inside. Paper sacks used to be the norm until the plastic bag came on the scene. Adding the handles made these easier to carry. The handles also made them easier to haul more and more stuff. What have you been hauling in your sacks? Is it trinkets from the flea market, meals from the local fast-food venue, or a wider and smarter TV? I'll admit, I've hauled a PBJ sandwich a time or two. A scrunched up fast-food bag has also been dragged from beneath my car seat. I've even hauled a television from the back seat of my car. But I've never taken $11,000 in a brown sack to the bank. Have you?

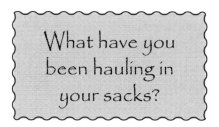

What have you been hauling in your sacks?

It's time for us to get a sack. For those who already have one, it's time to fill it wisely. It's time to get some strong sacks, not ones with holes in them, like the Old Testament Prophet Haggai spoke of in Haggai 1:6. It's time to stop stuffing our earnings in one end, only to have them seep out the other. A sack can hold a lot of earnings. Just ask the lady at the bank! An *un-holey* sack can *keep* a lot of earnings until time to use them wisely. It's time to believe that you, like my mom, are capable of taking an old paper sack to the bank.

Most choices in life have some sort of string attached, and that string is usually financial in nature and attached to our sacks. It's pretty obvious when someone is reaching inside from the top. We can easily spot them approaching, giving us time to shut the sack. It takes a keen eye to keep watch from the underside where unsuspecting pinholes can form. Before you know it, the holes have gotten larger, you've lost all your contents, and you haven't a clue where they went. This book is about keeping watch from above and below. It's about wisely choosing what we put in our sacks, pleasures for the moment or treasures for the future. It's about strengthening the walls of our bags to prevent pinholes from ever forming. We work too hard not to have something to show for it. We work too hard not to have a sizeable retirement fund for the future. Are we not one of, if not, the richest nation in the world?

Growing up, the thought of having a million dollars rarely crossed my mind, nor did I see the need, or have the fortitude, to obtain it. I've always been a lover of math ever since I can remember. My orange second-grade math book was one of my favorites. I carried my affinity for numbers well into high school where Mrs. Johnson introduced me to the joys of Algebra. (I know, I'm weird.) Not only did 1+2=3; I then learned that A+B=C! Having that knowledge may look great on a report card or high school transcript, but unless its application translates onto one's financial bottom-line, it's nothing more than numbers on a page. Throughout my schooling, I mastered the ABCs and 123s. But somewhere along the way, I missed the e-word: "exponential." I missed the higher mathematical function where time and compounding interest cause a current value to grow well beyond A+B+C. I missed the Rule of 72![2]

From Fire to Flakes

Financially speaking, I smell smoke, and I'm sounding the alarm on America's retirement crisis, beginning with my own. The brush fires in our lives are springing up all around, and we're waiting for a fire truck to arrive when the water hose is within our reach. If each of us doesn't stop the spread, we'll end up with a charred life and nothing to show for it. We must begin by debunking the lie that "time is money." Time is *not* money, else we'd all be gazillionaires! Time ticks away while money wastes away, and until we begin to value both precious commodities, they will continue to disappear before our eyes.

Where is the one place where fire cannot exist? In the snow! Snowbirds flee it every year because it piles up in mounds in front of their homes until their vehicles disappear in the driveway. Every mound starts with a flake, one measly flake. They fall one by one, but when they touch down, they can't be distinguished from another. Only the Creator sees the difference. These frozen crystals build and build until the original dusting becomes a thin layer of whiteness. Depending upon the size and time frame, that dusting turns into a sizeable accumulation that could amass a mound.

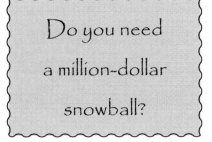
Do you need a million-dollar snowball?

In *Snowball Investing*, I invite you to build a snowball, a million-dollar snowball. How did I arrive at that number? Well, given that almost 10 years ago my Dad's in-home care was close to $10,000 per month, add some of that wonderful *e-liciously* exponential inflation, and we can agree on that figure doubling over the next 10 to 15 years. These numbers aren't in concrete, but they *are* pretty sticky. Now we're up to $20,000 per month. $20,000 x 12 months = $240,000 per year. Insurance companies are tracking these costs, along with the average length of time spent in assisted living and nursing home facilities. That's how they come up with their fine-tuned actuarial premium estimates. It's not that they don't love your Aunt Mabel; they just don't want to go broke paying for her to live.

Recent reports suggest that the average assisted-living stay lasts 28 months while more intensive nursing home care can almost match that time frame. So, if you total all of the estimated months (and insurance companies do), that's a little over 4 ½ years. Let that sink in.[3] If you're spending $240,000 every year x 4 ½ years, you might need to prepare for a $1,080,000 nest egg, minus your long term care policy benefits. That's how I arrived at a million-dollar snowball! (I told you I loved math.) And I shudder to think what the costs will be for a husband *and* wife.

So, there you have it. The handwriting's on the wall. It's time for action. We need to get busy, plug up our pinholes, and get to shoveling. It's 2018 and I am in the midst of my own snowstorm. Not literally, although I experienced one a few months ago. (More about that later.) But it makes no sense for me to wait until my million-dollar ball is done before I help you gather *your* flakes. There's been enough time melting away. Let's get going and build them together, encourage one another, and celebrate one another's successes in order to nudge others onto the slopes.

In this book there are times when I will be brutally honest. I will "come clean," so you can see where I've slipped; so hopefully you won't have to. I will reveal the hindrances to, and springboards towards, building a snowball. I will offer concrete strategies that you can begin to implement *today*. I've sprinkled stories of my life with humorous and serious accounts to help you remain laser-focused on the snowball goal, while fighting back the temptations that seek to steer us off course. I will provide charts and tables to help you gauge progress on your snowball-building. I will give hundreds of simple ways to save at least $1.00 per *year*. You will see how ridiculously easy that number can be raised in any budget. Lastly, I will conclude with an illustration of what true wealth and lasting riches are all about.

It's snowing. Are you ready to hit the slopes and start rolling out your million? Then suit up. Snowball-building is fun, but it can get awfully cold at times. You need to dress in layers to weather the frigid temperatures. Grab your cap and pull it snugly over your ears to drown out the naysayers. Insulate your fingers with waterproof gloves for the lengthy roll ahead. Strap on those galoshes to secure your every step. Grab a shovel to lift the weighty mounds along the way. Tilt your head back, feel the freshness of the snowflakes, and get to stepping. But don't forget your sack, a really big sack!

FREEZE! ●

What 3 purchases or spending habits keep poking pinholes in your sack?

1. _____
2. _____
3. _____

· TWO ·

Come Clean - Confess the Mess

I should have been a millionaire in the year 2011. Not because I have athletic or musical talents that launched me into a lucrative career. Not even because I've paired my love for math with the teachings of billionaire financial gurus from the 20th century. I own no beach front property that's tripled in value. I'm just an ordinary middle-class American with a couple of college degrees who, with the exception of a cumulative seven-month unemployment stint, has enjoyed the luxury of steady income throughout my entire working career. It hasn't even been one of extraordinary financial reward. In fact, most of those years were spent in the school system where many occupational therapists make the least amount of money in our profession. Yet, time has proven that it has been one of the safest havens during our country's economic upheavals.

So, what makes me think that a school system salary could have produced a million bucks? Simple: a little money steadily invested over a long period of time with a realistic rate of return equals a million. And why didn't it happen? A lack of accountability, a denial of the inevitable, an inconsistent plan (which is no plan at *all*), and a handful of idiotic wealth-building ventures.

> I should have been a millionaire in the year 2011.

What was *your* year? When did you lose *your* million? Or better yet, to whom was it gifted? Did you divvy it out on Madison Avenue, Bourbon Street, or Rodeo Drive? Most Americans, no matter their age, race, or economic status, have had financial slips-ups that have landed them flat on their backs. Most of mine have been meticulously outlined in Appendix A, so you'll understand that I've been on the same slippery slopes as you. (I know you "analytical minds" are flipping to the back of the book right now. You just can't resist numbers, can you?)

Plug the Holes

Growing up, I used to love to sing the song, "There's A Hole in My Bucket." It was short, it had just a few variations in the stanzas, and the ending was almost identical to the beginning.[4] This song has undergone a string of German-American versions over the past few centuries, with different names and scenarios interjected. The essence of the song is this: a husband (who I'll call *Harry*) states a problem with his bucket (namely, a hole in it.) His wife (who I'll name *Lizzie*) offers a solution to his problem. Each time Lizzie offers a solution, Harry comes up with an excuse for why it won't work. When Lizzie offers her final solution, Harry's reply is, "there's a hole in my bucket." (And around and around it goes…)

If you're a Type A personality, that song could drive you nuts. Your impatience might stifle your willingness to help Lizzie's husband Harry solve his problems. After all, he's the man of the house. He should be mechanically adept to fix his own bucket. Why bother Lizzie? She's got enough to do around the house!

What about us? We're holding our own buckets laden with holes with no Harry or Lizzie to help us. How in the world can we accumulate anything with such a useless tool? Before we can put our hands on a container and start storing our savings, we first need to debunk the excuses that punch holes in our buckets. Facing the giants takes honesty. Quite honestly speaking, if you're not willing to face this situation in a transparent manner, you will not succeed. So, let's look the giants in the mirror and begin working our way through the "hole-y" list.

> We're holding our own buckets laden with holes! How in the world can we accumulate anything with such a useless tool?

UNHOLEY HOLES IN ONE

Hole # 1 – I'm Overwhelmed and Tired
Welcome to the club. We all have our crosses to bear. Put the book down and get a good night's sleep. Start again tomorrow. Wake up, eat a good, healthy breakfast (balanced with protein, carbs and fats), do a lap around the cul-de-sac, fill a large water bottle to keep your brain hydrated, and start reading. If you know how to pray, pray! Have a highlighter nearby to mark the points that jump out at you. Once you see that there's a light at the end of the tunnel (and it's not the noonday train), your anxiety level should begin to recede.

Hole #2 - I Don't Know Where to Start
Everybody knows how much kids love snow. Even college kids love snowball fights. Adults just want to stay inside where it's warm. From a savings perspective, that could be deadly. If the heat being generated is coming from a furnace with carbon monoxide escaping, it could lull you to sleep. Inactivity can kill you. It's time to get out in the snow and build your snowball. The next chapter will show you how. I will share with you exactly what I did. Tweak it as you see fit. Just remember that you're aiming for a long-range goal, not a quick-fix solution.

Hole #3 – My Spouse Won't Cooperate

This may be the greatest challenge of all. I was able to start rolling out my snowball while I was still single, so I only had myself to contend with. (That was easy to do, once I realized I was lying face down in the snow and needed to get up before I got frostbitten.) When I did get married nine years ago, we had the makings of a miniature World War III brewing in the house for a while. Hubby thought I was trying to control his spending, while I was only trying to help *plan* his spending. It took him a while to see that my proposed budget was a format for giving, saving, *and* spending. He now will tell you that the plan has brought freedom in areas he never thought were possible. And one guess on who now manages the household budget!

If you happen to be matrimonially tied to an ornery mate who is as stubborn as a mule, your "war" may need a little more artillery. Help your spouse see the long-term benefits for both of you. Help them see that a little "no" in frivolous spending today can result in many "yeses" in intentional spending tomorrow, at a time when it will matter most. If your spouse is a visual learner, read this book together. If they won't sit still to do that, finish it yourself and develop a plan where both of you can experience long-term rewards. Using a friend's analogy, "paint the picture" so they see themselves benefitting in it. If they still won't get onboard, offer this short-term proposal: if you implement a plan and the family financials have not improved after six months, you will be open to hearing their solution. (This doesn't get them off the hook, it just gives them time to create their own plan.) If after all of this, your spouse is still not onboard, there's a deeper issue. Put the book on the shelf and head straight to your pastor, rabbi, or a strong counselor who is not afraid to provide "in your face" advice.

Hole #4 – My Kids Won't Cooperate

Keep reading. Margaret's and Megan's story will shed some light on what to do with your kids. Begin to teach them the value of generous giving, responsible spending, and systematic saving. Develop a work ethic in your kids at all ages so they will take responsibility for their financial choices, rather than looking to outside sources to shoulder their budgetary blunders. Begin to crack the hard shell of entitlement with your middle-schoolers and beyond. Give them spur-of-the-moment life lessons, such as buying groceries on *your* list with a set amount of cash (yes, I said cash), and rewarding them with a percentage of whatever they don't spend.

Hole #5 – I'm Too Broke

Join a second club! According to NerdWallet, the average household in America in 2017 carried almost $16,000 in credit card debt.[5] Given this statistic, you can figure out whether you fit into the "Little Bitty But It Ain't Pretty" indebted group, the "Average Old Joe" group, or the "Woe Is Me I'm In Big Trouble" group. No matter the group, I would venture to say you're ready to be excommunicated! No fear; help has arrived. Just remember the definition of insanity: doing the same thing over and over again, expecting different results. You've begun to make a change and the results can only get better, *if* you persevere. One quick Internet search and you'll find gobs and gobs of people from all walks of life who reached the boiling point and made a 180-degree turn in order to get their financial holdings in the black. Oh, distressed and bewildered one, can you not see yourself doing the same? Of course, you can!

Hole #6 – My Family and Friends Will Make Fun of Me

Will Rogers is quoted as saying, "*Too many people spend money they haven't earned, to buy things they don't want, to impress people they don't like.*" Unless these people are directly connected to your future well-being, I wouldn't give them a second thought.

My good friends, Maurice and Judy Payne, have spent over thirty years reaching out to senior citizens in Ringgold, Georgia, through their nursing home ministry, Forgotten Millions. I recently asked Brother Payne if, in all the years of moving in and out of nursing homes, he had ever heard loved ones make fun of their aging relatives' wise and fruitful financial decisions. This was his response:

> "*We usually don't get into any personal discussions about finances but we are sure no one ever regrets having prepared for their retirement. We do know that the folks that still have assets when they pass usually have family members that never came to see them in the nursing home but try to get their money. It seems most of the folks in assisted living homes have prepared well for their future or they couldn't live there because some are really costly. By the way, folks that we've met over 100 years old seem to be thriftier about it all.*"

If you still are antsy about stepping out and making a radical shift in your financial matters for fear of what others will say, I recommend Lou Priolo's book, *Pleasing People: How Not to Be an Approval Junkie*.[6] It offers the necessary guidance for plugging up this ridiculous hole. Lou's book is a no-holds-barred perspective on the addiction for approval from others and the only solution to rid oneself from its stronghold.

Hole #7 – I'm Too Old and It's Too Late

I just experienced a sad but startling reality: In a 15-minute internet search, I could not find *one* story about a senior citizen that got out of debt. Either none exists or the mass majority of financiers have surmised that this segment of the population is beyond help. I beg to differ. In fact, what kind of Christian would I be if I didn't care about the financial well-being of my fellow senior brothers and sisters and seek to help them? Debt is debt, no matter who has it, and the long-term effects are the same—devastation. Many seniors (those I'll define as 75 and above) will probably need our assistance to help meet their basic needs over an extended period of time. (All the more reason for

> "The second is this, 'You shall love your neighbor as yourself.' There is no other commandment greater than these."
>
> MARK 12:31

the rest of us to become debt-free.) I may not agree with the modern-day phrase, "It Takes A Village," since I don't know who's living in the village, but I can't wiggle around Jesus' command to "love my neighbor as myself" (Mark 12:31).

I have been listening to financial advisors over the years, and I always get a lump in my throat when I hear them seek to comfort a scared widow who's just lost her spouse of forty years and doesn't know what to do. It's those real-life moments that help me stay grounded. That could have easily been my mother on the other end of the phone. In fact, that could be *me* in another 30 years. (Of course, that would make me over 90, but remember, longevity runs in my family.)

Hole #8 – I Am in Debt Up to My Eyeballs

We all know the quickest way to eat an elephant: one bite at a time. We've all heard about taking baby steps. Baby steps are cute, but when you see an adult walking like that, it looks downright weird. Ladies and gentleman, getting out of debt in America looks weird. Delayed gratification is weird. Having more than $1000 in savings is weird.[7]

All in favor of being weird raise your hands high! *Snowball Investing* is written for the weirdos. The Average Joes have each other to lean on. I'm here for the rest of you. If your debt is up to your eyeballs, stand on your tippy toes and forge ahead. At least you're willing to see your way out of this mess instead of burying your head in the sand.

Hole #9 – Your Hole in One

What is your personal hole? What is your biggest deterrent? What's that one thing that wrecks every attempt to save? What vice do you have that saps your bank account on a whim? (And most of what we do is on a whim, isn't it?) What expense do you repeatedly justify that irks your spouse, soothes your cravings, and keeps you in the red? What spending is driven by an unrealistic guilt complex? Find a way to debunk it right now. You're going to have to feel your way through your own maze of monetary mayhem, so you might as well start here!

SNOWBALL SNIPPETS

What is your personal hole?

_____
_____
_____

What is your biggest deterrent?

_____
_____
_____
_____

What's that one thing that wrecks every attempt to save?

_____
_____
_____
_____

What vice do you have that saps your bank account on a whim?

1. _____
2. _____
3. _____
4. _____
5. _____

Before we head to the how-tos of this book, we need to hit two points hard. I'm concerned that Lizzie's husband Harry's mindset may still be lingering, and your bucket may still have a couple of leaks: denial of the future and flirtation with debt.

Denial of the Future

Whether you're a baby boomer, Generation Xer, millennial, or prefer to not be labeled, the inevitable needs to be faced. We all are either going to die young or die old. I'm sorry if that surprises you. If you think I'm making this up, ask your great-great grandfather. Whether you're young, middle-aged, old, or an old fogey, if you live long enough, you may not be able to take care of yourself. Even my friend's mother needed assistance before she went to heaven at the age of 108. That's pretty remarkable, isn't it? She spent her latter years helping the old folks! She was able to care for her basic needs but was beginning to slow down, so her son Hubert and daughter-in-law Robin lovingly moved her into their home until Jesus was ready for her.

But what if you don't have a Hubert and Robin? What if you can't keep going it alone, and need assisted living services or long-term nursing care? It costs! Costs are steadily rising, and it all may fall solely on your shoulders. Are you in denial about this? If you challenge my numbers, I challenge *you* to do one thing: Do an internet search of assisted living facilities in your neighborhood that are government-run, church-sponsored, and privately owned. Make an appointment to tour each one. (I just left a privately-owned one and it was posh!) There's nothing better than a road trip to give us a reality check. Yes, we're going somewhere. Isn't it time to build a snowball?

Flirting with Debt

I love to watch the black and white version of the science fiction movie, *The Blob*.[8] It begins with a man who sees something fall from the sky and goes to investigate it. The object glows and pulsates in the moonlight. Out of curiosity, the man takes a stick and pokes at it until it clings to the stick. He lifts it into the air for a closer glance. The substance slides down the stick, causing the man to flip it in the opposite direction. He does this a few times, flirting with the timing of the slippery slide, but the substance suddenly jumps onto his fingers and won't let go. It has his hand. It has his arm. The man realizes that he's in trouble and quickly seeks help from the hospital down the road. The attendees place him in a private room and leave him for just a short period. When they return, the small substance has grown and totally consumed the man. That little entity on the end of a stick kept growing and destroying everything in its path. It terrorized the entire town until the leaders devised a plan to rid themselves of it.

We all can be minding our own business and debt seems to fall from the sky. That's what happened to me in college. I was focused on completing my degree while a major credit card company had another plan.

Out of nowhere I was *gifted* with a precious little plastic card and a $500 credit limit. That was the beginning of the entity on my stick. It slid up and down until its tentacles attached to my hand in the form of charging stuff. It kept growing and growing until it consumed my world. The consumption had a name: *compounding interest.* Let's name it "CI." CI is designed to latch onto whomever flirts with it. CI slithers on a stick each month, waiting for unsuspecting prey to delay paying off the balance. Then CI latches on and brings more stickiness with it. CI grows and grows until it has your wallet by the throat.

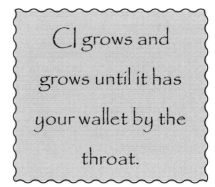

What's a victim to do? The same thing that those town leaders did. You must devise a *plan.* Piddly B-B gun pellets won't destroy it. Tanker artillery won't destroy it. You have to *freeze* CI and send it back into outer space where it belongs!

Do you have CI on a stick? Rather yet, does CI have *you*? Are you denying it's slithering power? Do you think you can juggle CI back and forth without it attaching itself to you? CI is from another world. You can't compete with it. You just can't…

If there is any inkling that CI lives in the recesses of your financial world, but you don't think it's doing much damage, I have a second assignment for you. It will only take a few seconds each day over the next week. You must follow my instructions precisely; otherwise, something might slip by. (No pun intended.)

Facing CI in the Face

1. Next Monday evening, gather the following coins and currencies: a dime, two one-dollar bills, one five-dollar bill, and one ten-dollar bill.
2. On Tuesday, while driving to work, roll down your window and toss the dime out the window. (If you work from home, toss it into the neighbor's yard. If you're in a condo, roll it down the hallway.)
3. On Wednesday, drop the one-dollar bill in the parking garage or place it under the neighbor's doormat.
4. On Thursday, flush the next one-dollar bill down the toilet.
5. On Friday, drop the five-dollar bill in the crack between the elevator doors, or stuff it in the cracks in the nearest sidewalk.
6. On Saturday, bless a stranger with the ten-dollar bill.
7. On Sunday, head to church and pray that I don't ask you to do this again next week!

Whether I ask you to repeat this or not, if you are an average American, you are literally doing this *every single week*. In June 2016, it was reported that the average American was wasting $855 per year *just* on credit card interest.[9] If you find yourself in this category, you are literally performing this little monetary annihilation each week of the year—**52 times per year!**)

Your hard-earned money is being tossed out the window, dropped in a parking garage, flushed down the toilet, stuffed down an elevator shaft, and handed off to strangers. And your solution on Sunday is what? *Lord, get me out of this mess!* I don't think He led you into it!

It's Monday morning. Did you have the guts to toss the coin? I hate losing coins, don't you? I hate losing $17.10 worth of coins, every week…year after year after year.

My grill-building, screwdriver-twisting, debt-destroying plan absolutely will not have *any* impact in your life until the blob is frozen. Killed. Sent back into outer space. Enough said. Let's get out in the snow.

FREEZE! ●

Does CI have its tentacles wrapped around your wallet? ☐ Yes ☐ No

Are you ready to freeze CI today? ☐ Yes ☐ No

Make the Commitment! Write the date and time.

_____

· THREE ·

A Bell, A Blizzard, and A Budget

I braced myself as the touchdown triggered two giant thumps. The roar of the engine outside my window quickly diminished to a whistling sound. The screeching of brakes beckoned the aircraft to stop, while lights whisked by in the backdrop of the night's air. Anthony and I gathered our luggage and headed towards the carrier's door, up the jetway, and straight to the car rental counter. Moments later, as we rolled our bags across the airport exit threshold, my eyelids moistened from sweet memories of the past. My lips could not contain what had laid dormant in my heart. I inhaled the crisp, cool air of Colorado Springs and shouted, "I'm home!"

So, what were we doing in this part of the country, and why was I calling Colorado Springs *home*? An eight-month job assignment in northern New Mexico, almost two decades beforehand had produced more than a paycheck. It had produced a lifetime of friendships, and this trip was long overdue.

The planning of this trip began with a simple social media post by my friend, Mike (my former pastor from New Mexico). He was on a mission trip to China, and I begged him to bring me a souvenir bell to add to my international collection. A week later, his message stated that he had the bell and wanted to know where to mail it. My reply was, "I'll come and get it!" So, Anthony and I began our cross-country trip for a simple bell and an overdue reunion with dear friends.

Mike and his wife, Chrissie, welcomed us as overnight guests. The next day, after a Colorado-style breakfast, retrieval of the prized possession, and a short excursion around the Springs, we traveled south to reconnect with the New Mexico townspeople. Anthony and I received hearty welcomes from so many of them, including Charlie and Isabel Gonzales, owners of Zellers Cleaners. As we chatted near their picture window at the corner of Second Street and Apache Avenue, a soft snow began to fall. The Gonzales' remarked that the area hadn't experienced any moisture (rain or snow) for eight months, so this shower was gladly received.

An Expected Forecast
As the moments passed and flakes began to cover our windshield, Charlie recalled a blizzard that had blanketed the interstate years before. He and Isabel gave a mutual nod that it had been a harrowing time in the region. Given our afternoon plans, this was *not* the story I wanted Anthony to hear. Friends in

the nearby town of Des Moines (37 miles east) were expecting our arrival; after all, a huge after-school gathering had been planned!

Just as quickly as the snow accumulation began, the flakes stopped falling, the clouds lifted, and within minutes, the sun had melted almost every trace of the frozen dusting. That was our cue to wrap up the picture-taking, say our final goodbyes, and set our car wheels on the Clayton Highway.

A panoramic view, sprinkled with a tapestry of clouds, engulfed our car on both sides. Anthony enjoyed the view while I enjoyed the memories. It felt so surreal that an African-American woman would be so eager to return to such a desolate place. Yes, I loved the scenery and the serenity of it all, but in less than an hour, I would be reminded once again why I loved the people so much.

Our arrival at the front office coincided with school's dismissal. While students filed past, word quickly spread that the Smith's had arrived, and scores of familiar faces began to trickle from the back halls. After a barrage of bear hugs and a whirlwind tour of the new buildings, teachers scurried around to lock up and make their way to the Sierra Grande restaurant down the road. Conversations around the table ranged from cattle to classrooms to rattlesnakes. (Thank the Lord I didn't encounter the latter while I lived there!) Our quaint little reunion lasted more than an hour, littered with fond memories and catching up on everyone's present lives.

Halfway into the meal, the scene outside our window started to resemble the one at the Cleaners. The snow had followed us to Des Moines, and it was falling fast and fiercely. I thought it was absolutely beautiful. Anthony thought it was a blizzard in the making. He knew the path we had traveled to get there; a path without hotels, gas stations, or rest stops. We were in big ranch territory, so dwellings were few and far between.

After Anthony nudged me under the table for the third time, I conceded that it was finally time to depart. We took our final pictures, shared our final hugs, and headed out the door. Anthony slid behind the wheel and we buckled up, preparing for our lengthy ride home.

A Blizzard in the Making

The snow was breathtaking but blinding. The beaming headlights offered little relief in guiding our path. Strong winds hurled flakes sideways with more intensity than in Raton; only this time, they were not letting up. All we could see was white: the air, the mountains, and the ground. We rode in silence, careful not to utter our mutual concern of not making it back. While Anthony kept the wheels within the lane, I monitored temperature readings from my phone. We were hovering around 36 degrees; a narrow cushion above freezing, but a cushion nonetheless.

Each minute inched us closer to our safe and secure hotel room, but the conditions were not improving. I began to question my reluctance to leave earlier. I wondered if we might hit an icy spot and spin out of control. Would this be another déjà vu moment like the one I experienced on this same stretch many years before? On that cold blistery morning I headed to work, not knowing that the superintendent had delayed school opening by two hours. Driving along the highway, I suddenly found myself in a winter wonderland of ice, forcing me to reduce the car's speed, and praying that I'd make it safely in.

One quick blink, and my thoughts returned to the car with Anthony. We rode for miles as the snow relentlessly continued to stick. Anthony's eyes stayed glued to the road while mine stayed glued to the phone. Thirty-six degrees brought little comfort, considering what we saw ahead of us. As we passed the city road sign, our hearts sank in a synchronized sigh. Raton was *still* 27 miles away, and we had only traveled a third of the distance. Silent prayers went forth. *Lord, let us make it back safely.*

If I hadn't seen it with my own eyes, I wouldn't have believed the next turn of events. We were still on the same highway we had been traveling for the previous twenty minutes; yet, in a matter of seconds, the entire scene changed from all white to all brown. Not a gradual change, an *instantaneous* change, as if someone had flipped a dimmer switch. We must have cleared a spot surrounded by mountains that had held the frozen moisture in the atmosphere. We both breathed a sigh of relief, grateful that we wouldn't have to endure anymore blizzard conditions. And Anthony was grateful that we wouldn't be stranded on a stretch of road littered with more wildlife than people!

So, what in the world do a bell and blizzard have to do with a budget? For me, it was the pursuit of a bell that landed me in the middle of two blizzard-like conditions. The first one was predicted; it began as a trickle and piled up quickly, but the sun caused it to vanish in a short time. The second one was also predicted but resembled a blizzard. It fell suddenly, accumulated quickly, and blanketed the area; but it didn't last either.

Snowflakes come and go. Sometimes they're just a light sprinkling that graze the surface of your face. Sometimes they fall steadily, inciting a visible accumulation. When they expand in size and frequency, the gentle snowfall turns treacherous with no end in sight. From a financial perspective, whether you're blundering the debt blob or rolling out a million-dollar snowball, ***every flake counts***. And the melting away or the piling up of snowflakes can directly impact your budget.

The flakes are in your paycheck. You may only have a visible dusting. You may experience a sizeable pile-up. You may even encounter an occasional blizzard from a bonus, lump-sum pay raise, or income tax refund. These are all useable flakes for future savings.

I can hear some of you protesting: "My flakes dissolve so quickly that I can't grasp or see them, much less am able to put them to use." My dear financier, close your eyes, take a deep breath, and imagine the roar of snow plows. The next 15 chapters contain hundreds of flakes that you may be overlooking. They may have brushed against your face, but somehow, you've managed to overlook their presence. It's time to get traction on this journey. I'm here to shore you up and help you to experience financial frostbite while you pick up countless snowflakes along the way. Be encouraged; each flake-capturing moment will be worth it!

Footprints in the Snow - The Plan

In this book, you have a twofold task to perform with your snowflakes. First, you must identify and use them to bring your debt balance to **zero** (excluding your mortgage), and you must do this as quickly as possible. You must take every flake that you can find and apply it to blob busting. This is the action that will skim months and even years off your indebtedness. It worked for me and it can work for you. Once you eliminate your debt, you can then begin to use those same financial flakes the very next month to begin rolling out your investment snowball. You will soon discover that snow accumulates faster when debt is not melting it away! Also, keep in mind that it's perfectly fine with me if you take on additional work to roll the process even faster. So, are you ready to make footprints and get some traction started? Here we go!

> Bring your debt balance to $0 as quickly as possible to keep your assets from melting away!

Budget to Zero

Before we begin, I need to reiterate one point: living on credit will create a perpetual meltdown. My definition of credit is *imaginary money used to fulfill unrealistic wants, needs, and desires*. You cannot and will not ever advance in snowball-building without the use of *real* dollars, *real* cents, and real *common* sense. If you are using credit cards to pay any of the necessities of life (food, shelter, gas, and utilities), things are more critical than you can imagine. But all hope is not lost. Your financial picture can begin to get brighter today, just as mine did one Saturday morning in 1984. (More about that later.) It started with one piece of paper that contained words and lines; it was a budget form. Now, before burying your head in the snow, hear me out. Budgets have gotten a bad rap. They've been labeled as the enemy, and we avoid them like the plague. Quite frankly, they *really* are our friend. They're like a magnifier, an eraser, a hammer, and a key. They highlight our earnings, expose the devouring leeches in order to eliminate them, break up the credit chaos, and help us start the engine towards systematic wealth-building.

A sample budget form is located in Appendix B. Use the one I've developed or select one from the Resources List to complete all categories pertaining to you and your family. **Make several copies before**

you begin for future revisions. (You can also download a copy from my website, www.snowball-investing.com or my *Snowball Investing* Facebook® page.) Complete the form in the following manner:

- Start by listing your monthly take-home income at the top. Then begin to work through the priority categories. Those include items such as giving, housing costs, reasonable groceries, utilities, and car expenses. On each line, insert the amount that you currently spend (within reason). If you have an erratic take-home pay such as income from commissions, total your earnings from the last 12 months and divide by 12 to arrive at an estimated monthly income.

- Next, fill in all outstanding debt categories. Yes, that means those dastardly credit card payments, along with school debt, personal loans, etc.

- If you already have $1200 in savings, you can skip this third step. Otherwise, you need to make an entry for *911 Savings*. It will come when least expected, like when the home's original air-conditioning dies in July, or when your rental house's furnace goes kerplunk in January. (This really happened!) Plug in a monthly amount between $100-200. **Draw a circle around the "911 Savings" entry so you will not forget it.** You will need to revisit this as you near the form's completion. The goal is to accumulate $1200 ASAP, but you first need to see how the rest of the budget shakes out. You may be able to increase this monthly amount with any surplus funds. (By the way, I arrived at a $1200 *911 Savings* amount because every time there's an emergency, it seems to cost $1000, plus some specialty bolt, nut, or over-priced washer. Am I right?)

- Make sure you fill in an amount in the **Unexpected Expense Savings** entry. Your goal will be to save 40-50% of your take-home pay for any huge expenditures in the future. These could be as gloomy as a legal expense or as favorable as a timely all-cash vehicle purchase.

- Now that the priority monthly obligations have been entered, it's time to **budget to zero**. Plug the monthly take-home salary into your calculator. Then begin to subtract each **essential** budgeted entry. After you have deducted all monthly essentials, you are left with an amount to use for the remaining categories. (Notice, I didn't start with entries such as entertainment. That's labeled as **frivolous** spending when you're in a financial drought.) Enter *reasonable* amounts in the remaining categories, from the most important to the least.

- When you reach the end of the categories, rejoice if you have even *one dollar* left. That represents a flake. That represents the makings of a snowball. More will accumulate, especially as you eliminate the debts. At least you're not functioning in the red.

- If you *are* functioning in the red, it's okay. I've been where you are. I've played the game of mailing the utility check two days before payday, knowing that by the time the check cleared the bank, I had next month's paycheck already deposited. Playing the "race against time" game was no game, and no fun. When I embraced that precious budget form and took it to heart, the fat was trimmed from spending (although things were already pretty lean), and within two weeks, I was coincidentally asked to provide private therapy to a client on a weekly basis. (A coincidental offer to earn extra income? I think not. A gift from the Lord, no doubt!) At this point, review each category's entry and trim some *more* fat until you have spent all of your paycheck and you're in the **black**. That's what it means to "Budget to Zero." If there's any extra money after everything is covered, hold on; it has a purpose.

- If, after the previous step, you are still in the red, look in the mirror and ask yourself, "Am I still sitting on some fat?" (I don't mean in a literal sense!) Are you engaged in week-day shopping, weekend tripping, and year-long reckless living that comes with a price tag? Get up, get out the machete, and cut the fat 'til it hurts! If you have taken an honest look at spending and you're not ordering Friday night pizzas or upgrading electronic devices on a whim, but things are still in the red, there is *still* hope, and it's only pages away! Black will come sooner than you ever imagined **if** you're ready to make a color change.

- Once your budget is in the black, revisit it every quarter to reassess your progress and make any necessary adjustments. It will be an encouraging and tangible sign that debt-busting *does* work! Ask a trusted friend to hold you accountable to living within your means; a friend who has a disdain for debt, not a love for Black Friday!

- Take a short break. Things are fixin' to get down-right dirty.

 FREEZE! •

Make a commitment to stick to your budget.
Name the friend who you believe will hold you accountable.

_____

· FOUR ·

Millions in the Mud

No matter where you are on your financial journey, pretty soon you're going to have to get down and dirty to make your plan work. An interesting thing happened last year to remind me of this. Anthony and I *once again* decided that a particular Friday would be *financial organization* day. We would pull out our investment summaries, review gains and losses, and invest the available funds that had gone uninvested for months. The night before, I suggested that we go out for a relaxing breakfast before tackling this venture, to which he promptly agreed.

The next morning, we rose early and made our way to the neighborhood breakfast joint. The meal was great, the conversation was uplifting, and the service was fairly swift. As we pulled out of the restaurant parking lot, Anthony announced that he would run by the car wash before heading home. *Oh boy, here goes our day of financials being dwindled away by Friday errands.* I rolled my eyes but conceded to the morning's slight detour. At least the car wash was on the way home, so it couldn't eat up too much time.

Hubby pulled into the car wash, paid the attendant, put the car in neutral, and the swish-swash began. When we exited the other end of the bay, he made a quick right towards the vacuuming and window-washing area. It had been years since I had washed a car, so I forgot about the detailing involved. *Patience, Pat, patience.* I jumped out when Anthony was ready to remove the floor mats. I watched him vacuum his side of the car; then he came around to do my side. I quickly hopped back inside and waited for him to finish the rest. All of a sudden, in the middle of his window washing, he casually announced that pennies were lying all over the ground. That news catapulted me out of my seat, causing me to scurry all around our car. He was right. Pennies and more pennies! Shiny ones. Corroded ones. Some rested amidst the limbs and debris. I stooped and began retrieving these untimely finds. It turned out that some weren't even pennies! I moved from one stall to another. *Why were they here? Who opens their pockets and drops coins when vacuuming is free?* That's when Anthony informed me that people shake out their mats and let the

> Pretty soon you're going to have to get down and dirty to make your plan work.

coins drop on the ground. As I made my way down the curb, stooping every other second to retrieve these unexpected treasures, it occurred to me: *If any of these coins have been here awhile, perhaps some have gotten brushed <u>underneath</u> the ground coverings.* Sure enough, I planted my foot on piles of pine-straw and mud, and began to sweep them aside, exposing the treasures underneath. Oh, the joy of discovering pennies, nickels, and dimes, discarded by ordinary folks who devalued their worth. Anthony finished his feat, and I finished mine. My palms overflowed! I couldn't wait to get home and count them. The final tally was $1.30, lying on the ground, in the mud; stepped over by unassuming patrons. No regard for the lesser things.

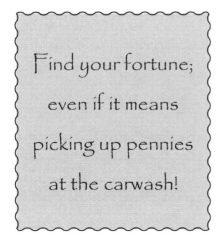

Find your fortune; even if it means picking up pennies at the carwash!

Saving for the future can be a drag. It may even feel like drudging through mud. I encourage you to start stepping anyway. Start by clearing away the dirt and debris that's clouding your ability to find your future savings. You may have to stoop to find it. You may have to dig a little deeper in your wallet. You may even have to slide some unnecessary expenses out of the way to make room for the essential ones. Whatever it takes, get going, keep going, and resist *not* going. Find your fortune; even if it takes brushing away pine-straw at the car wash. A millionaire once told me that he *never steps over a penny.* (Thanks, John, for that advice.) And the next time Anthony wants to go by the car wash, this lady won't be rolling her eyes, except to glance under the nearest pile of debris.

Unearthing the Mud

At this juncture, you either get to sigh or smile. If your budget is in the **red**, has *any* debt obligations, or you do not have fully funded *911 Savings* and *Unexpected Expense Savings* accounts, you are required to work this entire chapter before moving on. If your budget is in the **black** with no outstanding debt (besides a possible home mortgage), and you have fully funded *911 Savings* and *Unexpected Expense Savings* accounts, feel free to smile and skip to the next chapter to get the snowball rolling.

WORK THE PLAN

Get Started

To begin this process, you'll need to gather a few important tools. Check them off as you gather them:

- ☐ pencils
- ☐ erasers
- ☐ highlighter
- ☐ legal pad
- ☐ calculator (again)

Wad Through the Mud

Now that you've seen the enormity of your mud pile, it's time to start rinsing it away. It'll take more than a water hose, but it can be done. This is what I did years ago, and it still works today.

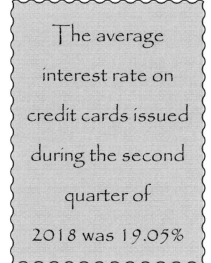

The average interest rate on credit cards issued during the second quarter of 2018 was 19.05%

Arrange the muddy debt pile from smallest to largest according to the outstanding balances.

Using the blank "Muddy Mess©" form, complete the following for each debt, working from left to right in each column:

- In column one, write the source of each debt, e.g., "Aunt Eleanor," or "Main Street Credit Card."

- Next, list the current balances since your last payment.

- List the current interest rate.

- At this point, in order to calculate your **Real Debt**, you need to add the blob to the mud: compounding interest (**CI**). Remember, it's still attached to your hand. It keeps showing up month after month. It won't go away until you get rid of it in its entirety. Since neither of us knows how fast you're going to tackle your debts, you must add some projected amount of interest that you will pay until it's gone. Add anywhere between 10% and 20% to the balance amount. (Keep in mind that the average interest rate on credit cards newly issued as of the second quarter of 2018 was 19.05%.) [12]

<u>Example</u>: Overpriced Electronics balance of $1200 x 10% = **$120**.
Balance amount ($1200) + Interest ($120) = **$1320**. This is the **Real Debt**, and it could go higher if it's not paid off within a year!

I know, you're screaming right now, "*That's not the balance on my statement.*" In all honesty, it *is*, if you allow the balance to linger for a year. And, that's not including the late fees, potentially higher interest rates, and creditor's fees if they have to come knocking for the full amount! Remember, blobs don't let go. Let this column sink in. That's the hole in the bucket. That's the hole in the brown sack. That's the monster from outer space.

- List any late fees that you could incur due to late payments. (This is just a visual reminder to help you stay on track.)

- List your monthly payment amount.

- Divide the **Real Debt** balance by the **monthly** payment to determine **the number of months remaining** for a total payoff.

  <u>Example</u>: Overpriced Electronics balance of $1320 divided by a monthly payment of $100 = 13.2 months for total payoff. (Round **down** to the whole number since you plan to accelerate payments, right?)

- Pull out the month-by-month yearly calendars. Starting with **next** month, count **forward** to determine the projected month and year for paying off each debt. (Don't get bogged down on the debts that you haven't been paying off each month. Just list them.)

 <u>Example</u>: The current month is **December 2018**. Total Overpriced Electronics balance is **$1320**, with 13 months of payments. January to December 2019 equals 12 months, plus one more (**January 2020**) equals **13 months**. The Mud-Free Date for Overpriced Electronics payoff would be **January 2020.**

- Identify the debt that will take the longest to pay off and highlight its date. That will be your total **Mud-Free Celebration Date!** That's the day when the mud is gone and you can begin your million-dollar snowball. And the coins in the mud piles, the coins that were previously wasted but have now turned into valuable dollars, is what you will use to freeze the blob and start the snowball rolling.

Well done. Give yourself a pat on the back. You have faced the alien!

FREEZE! •••

How many credit cards are in your household?   _____

How many are you ready to cut up today?   _____

Aren't you tired of the mud?   ☐ Yes   ☐ No

· FIVE ·

Expected Showers

Not one of us owns a cloud in the sky. We can't even hold or reach one. Only the Creator of clouds knows how thick they are.

"Do you know how God establishes them, and makes the lightning of His cloud to shine? Do you know about the layers of the thick clouds, the wonders of one perfect in knowledge..." (Job 37:15-16 NASB). Okay, so we don't own the clouds; we can all agree on that point. But we all *do* know what comes out of them. Our universal problem is that we can't always sync the forecast from the clouds with the outcome on earth.

Completing college at the Medical College of Virginia (MCV) was grueling at times. Our program's class of 25 bonded together, as we endeavored to complete our junior and senior years on the urban Richmond campus. Since MCV was built around old historic buildings, the campus was sprawled over several blocks in no defined pattern. One classroom building could be situated next to the city library or a major department store. And since all classroom buildings needed to be close to the MCV Hospital System, dormitories were located several blocks away. Needless to say, we students had to plan ahead on what was needed for the entire school day to avoid walking back and forth during precious break times.

I'll never forget that bright, sunny morning, when I was preparing for the day. The trek to my first class would start soon after breakfast, and classes wouldn't break until well past noon. I usually had the television on while getting dressed, and this morning was no different. The weatherman said there was a 30% chance of rain. Being the numbers person that I am, I sized up his forecast: If 50% is a coin's-toss, then 30% is far less than that. I wouldn't need to lug around an umbrella if the man was right. A few hours later I stepped out of the classroom building at East 11th and Marshall Streets. The man was wrong. It wasn't raining, it was pouring! Thirty-percent worth. Less than a coin's toss. *Way* less. Coin tosses leave you holding your breath. Thirty-percent leaves you drenched.

That happened almost 40 years ago. But even today, when I hear a forecast for rain and the weatherman says not to expect much with a 30% chance, I roll my eyes, rehearse my story with every nearby listening ear, and grab the umbrella. The weatherman is *never* 100% right. Can we all agree on that? He can't even detect where the wind goes, much less, what's inside of a cloud! "The wind blows where it wishes, and you hear the sound of it but do not know where it comes from and where it is going..." (John 3:8 NASB).

We can also agree that there *will* be weather, only we're not sure to what degree. We have a saying in Atlanta: "If you don't like the weather, wait five minutes." The meteorologist predicts sunshine while it's storming outside. He predicts a dusting of snow while you watch the neighborhood kids smash your windshield with a humongous snowball. We ladies prance around in our sundresses, only to dash into the closest department store at noonday because the temperature never reached 70 degrees. Things in the atmosphere change too quickly to predict. Nevertheless, we must be prepared for all conditions. That goes for the weather as well as our finances.

Snow in the Forecast

Planning for the future is a smart thing to do, but not necessarily an easy thing. Several years ago, I picked up a book entitled, *Smart Couples Finish Rich.*[13] Alas! This would be my husband's and my foolproof method for tackling the financials in a simple and systematic manner! I was especially drawn to the author's priority of helping the reader identify his or her value system and letting that be the driving force for investment planning. We were on our way, sailing through the chapters, agreeing on core values and what we wanted to accomplish for ourselves and for those significant in our lives. We eagerly welcomed the chapter that advised us to gather all important documents and store them in one central location for easy access.

Between Anthony's single file drawer and my massive four-drawer cabinet, we had plenty of storage. It was just a matter of locating and yanking out those forms on the author's list and checking them off. Oh, how I love checklists. They give me such a sense of accomplishment! According to the book's instructions, this crucial step should take only two days. We agreed to give ourselves *three*, since we were in the midst of juggling so many other things in our lives.

Someone once said that life was not easy. I wholeheartedly agree. Neither is gathering important papers! Never mind that I had purchased a box of brightly-colored yellow file folders and labeled every tab. It took *months* to check off that list. *Months!* That's when I realized why many couples don't make headway in resolving everyday family matters, much less tedious financial matters. You have to all but turn into a rhinoceros, put your head down, and purpose to plow through the daily grind to complete a task. I'll have to admit, the energy it took to complete just this one task left us both exhausted. Yes, every document was located. Yes, every folder was filed in alphabetical order. They all were stored in one central location like the directions called for; but we were mentally and physically spent, and it took *years* for us to even muster up the strength to open that book again!

I empathize with your struggles. Whether you are in the midst of duct taping holes in a sack, transitioning from red to black, or sobbing over a litany of muddy messes, the remaining chapters should encourage you. Most of us may have to go through the mud to get to the slopes. I did! Some of my mud piles just skimmed the surface. Some were quite watery. Many felt knee-deep, and at times I thought some would cause me to lose my footing and take me under. When it felt like things were overwhelming and at a stand-still, I had to pull out my debt-busting chart and view the progress. You may have to do likewise.

Bring on the Flakes
I've held you in suspense long enough. The temperature's dropped. The clouds have rolled in. The air is heavy. You just stepped outside to get the mail and something cool wet the tip of your nose. There it goes again. It's snowing! It's finally snowing! One flake at a time! Chapters 6 through 20 are loaded with snowflakes. Some are huge, while others are just light dustings. But isn't every snow mound nothing more than a whole lot of little flakes stuck together?

Each snowflake-building chapter is identified by a category of spending (such as *Travel* or *Food*). Your assignment is to read each chapter's list of items, and identify those areas where you are willing and able to save. These lists are not exhaustive by any means, so feel free to tailor them to your lifestyle and the expenses related to it. Keep in mind that *lifestyle* may be the catalyst that led you into the mud in the first place! It's time to get you *and* your money loosed.

As you read through the lists, you will see a line placed to the left of each entry. This is where your calculator comes in handy. On each line, write the number of dollars **per year** that you are willing to save on that entry. For example, if you purpose to save $5 per month on eating out, multiply that by 12 to achieve a $60 annual savings. Factor each entry on an **annual** basis versus monthly, because some expenses, such as getting an oil change, do not occur every month. An oil change savings, for example, may total a one-time $10 annual savings (from a coupon or other form of discount), so there's no need to do a monthly calculation.

Each category's chapter has blank lines at the bottom of the list. On those lines, fill in your own unique snowflake-saving ideas and the amounts you are willing to save per year. If you can think of multiple ideas, include those on the page. Add as many lines as you wish. The more flakes the merrier. Then total each chapter's amounts to obtain a potential **annual** savings. Enter each chapter's annual savings total on the *Snowflake Accumulation Worksheet*. Once all of the chapters have been completed, add them together on the form for the **Grand Annual Total**. Divide the *Grand Annual Total* by 12 to determine the *monthly* savings amount. This is the dollar amount that you can begin to apply towards blob-busting and *911/ Unexpected Expense Savings*, provided you're not padding your budget with the use of credit. **(That's why credit won't allow this equation to work.)** This number is also the size of your initial snowball, the amount that you will roll into investments every month (once your emergency categories are totally funded.) This is the amount that will grow exponentially with time and compounded interest. This is the beginning of your million-dollar snowball.

One major debt-busting rule: Those of you who still have debt are only allowed to make entries on line-items related to *reducing* current expenditures, *not* figuring out ways to cut additional expenses in *half!* Forget the notion of saving 50% on a low-peak season Orlando entertainment trip. That shouldn't even be on your debt-busting radar! Plan your next *"stay-cation"* with a water-play oscillating sprinkler and hotdogs on the grill, or indoor camping under grandma's quilt, suspended over two dining room chairs. **Stay put** until that budget is in the black!

Tracking the Snow Pile-Up

It's one thing to accumulate snow. It's another to roll it in the right direction. With all of the effort that you've put forth, the last thing we want to have happen is for those precious snowflakes to fall through the cracks. We've plugged up all holes; now we're about to plug up the cracks! All of that surplus that you'll accumulate each month needs to be tracked in writing (or a typed format.) We baby boomers are old enough to remember those leather-bound financial ledgers with sheets of green paper and a myriad of columns for every category known to man. In this case, you only need to track a few things: **the date, the nature of the transaction, the deposit or withdrawal/expense amount, and the balance.** Make several copies of this form, *Category Running Balance Worksheet©*, or download a copy from my online sites. You can even make your own! Just make sure that all of the columns are included.   A sample of the completed form is included, demonstrating how your transactions should be tracked each month. You'll need a form for each category. Yes, I said each! If you don't track 'em, you'll lose 'em. Your flakes will dissolve into the atmosphere and you won't know where they went. This will also uncover millions from the mud that you can transfer to your *Unexpected Expense Savings* category, as well as that long-awaited *Investment* category, on your Budget Form.

> The valuable tools for wealth building are among us: income, insurance, stocks, bonds, mutual funds, and everything in between!

Help on the Ski Slope

Snowball builders, may I offer one more valuable piece of advice before you head outside? While you are finding those precious flakes, take some time to learn about parts of a financial portfolio. If you're like me, you've gotten bits and pieces of the puzzle in your lifetime, leaving you totally frustrated, financially unstable, and not knowing which way to turn. The valuable tools for wealth-building are among us: income, insurance, stocks, bonds, mutual funds, and everything in between! But without proper guidance and understanding, it's too easy just to do *nothing*; and that approach won't get you prepared for the future, will it? So, shore up your own knowledge. Learn the lingo, or at least enough to ask intelligent questions when you begin to seek professional advice. Otherwise you'll be at the mercy of the one on the other side of the table. I don't want you to end up making future decisions that could further muddy the financial waters. (And you *know* how I feel about mud!)

SNOWBALL SNIPPETS

Take some time to learn about parts of a financial portfolio. Without proper guidance and understanding, it's too easy just to do **nothing**, isn't it?

What resources have you found?

_____
_____
_____
_____
_____
_____
_____
_____
_____
_____
_____

What aspects of investing do you need to learn about?

1. _____
2. _____
3. _____
4. _____
5. _____

· SIX ·

Beauty: *The Big Rip-Off*

I still remember that day. Althea was a friend and newly trained instructor at one of Atlanta's prestigious beauty schools. She had invited me to come and experience some of the fineries in the world of aesthetics. I had never given myself permission to indulge in things like French manicures, pedicures, and deep facial exfoliations; so, this was my moment. I scheduled my appointment for the works. Knowing that Althea would supervise all treatments, all I had to do was show up, sit back, and be pampered for a fraction of the cost.

> "The best and most beautiful things in the world cannot be seen or even touched - they must be felt with the heart."
> Helen Keller

Upon arrival, I was greeted by a very professional receptionist. We reviewed the treatments that I had previously selected, and I was then ushered into a private room to be prepped. I settled into a cushiony chair and was slowly reclined to a comfortable angle. Within a short time, the aesthetician intern entered the room and began to do her magic. My facial muscles were gently massaged, followed by a plush mildly-scented warm towel draped over my face. While the intern set the timer, I laid back with my eyes closed, basking in the warmth of the towel, and feeling myself gradually drift into a state of tranquility.

When the timer faintly dinged, the intern replaced the towel with another warm substance which she carefully smoothed beneath my brows, down the sides of my face, and underneath my chin. I felt myself slip further into that peaceful zone. She reached for a dry towel and wiped away the moisture, being careful to remove all traces of the substance. Oh, the touch. Oh, the pampering. Oh, the experience. Just as quickly as that substance was removed, another one was applied right above my lips. Such warmth. Such smoothness. Such *OUCH!* What just happened? No one prepared me for this! My state of euphoria was just ripped off by a wax job, setting my facial nerves on edge. The pain was over just as soon as it began, but this little jewel of torture was about to happen on the other side. I braced myself for the inevitable. Ripped again. I survived the ordeal and left with a glowing complexion, but nobody told me the whole story.

We all know the clichés: "Beauty is in the eye of the beholder." "Beauty's only skin deep." I prefer the words by Helen Keller: "The best and most beautiful things in the world cannot be seen or even touched - they must be felt with the heart."[14] I'd venture to say that the Beauty Industry would probably recoil at her words. Whichever quote you claim as your mantra, beauty is alive and well in America. Obtaining it costs, maintaining it is costlier, and once it begins to slip, sustaining it is most costly. In fact, in 2017, Americans spent well over $17.7 billion in this industry.[15]

Some of us may view beauty costs as luxury items. That's why I've combined them with toiletries, a necessity with which most would agree. We cannot ignore the need for the basics such as toothpaste, lotion, and deodorant. If we do, everyone within two feet of us will know it! But making the decision on these items *alone* can keep us scanning store aisles for hours.

Hair care options are numerous as well, with their ever-changing trends: the straight look, the curly look, the spiked look, the textured look. Cuts, trims, and waves. Almost every verb known to man is a hair technique. The black hair care industry by itself is so vast that comedian Chris Rock did a documentary on the topic.[16] I didn't see all of it, but the excerpts I saw were hilariously serious. Don't ever come between a black woman and her hair!

So, what's a budgeteer to do when there's a justifiable need for lipstick, lotion, and layers of curls? All we can do is make the wisest selections possible, search high and low for bargains, use equally effective homemade potions, and pray that these changes leave wiggle room for a beautiful net worth. After all, down the road we may still have a few teeth left to brush and a few strands of hair to curl.

My line items in this category may not exactly apply to your household, so modify them accordingly. Scratch through what doesn't work and fill in your specific needs. Whatever you do, keep going. Don't pull your hair out over it! And the next time you peruse the store aisles, try not to get ripped off!

My Gold for Others' Glory

Have you ever heard of Aigner®? Don't rush to do a Google® search on the name. Do you know the person? I didn't know either, but when I was a teenager, I felt pretty special when I finally was able to afford a pair of those stunning burgundy pumps with the signature horseshoe-shaped "A" on the side. They instantaneously improved my posture when I strutted with head held high and shoulders back, just like my mama taught me. Those shoes were special because they were *designer* shoes. They were the only designers that crossed my path during those years, so they were extra special. We Central Virginians shopped at towering department stores, like Richmond-based Thalheimers and its down-the-street rival, Miller and Rhoads. Each store spanned an entire city block. Back then, anything worthy enough to hang from their racks or occupy their shelves was considered high quality. So, to be able to acquire a pair of Aigner's from one of these icons set me a step above the rest.

Shoes are hard to find in my size. They were then, and they are now. Some women would consider that a curse. It's really a blessing. Had I been gifted with a size 7 foot, I wouldn't be writing a book on building an investment snowball, but on unloading an avalanche of shoes. No doubt, in today's world with its innumerable supply of footwear, my closet would be running over with every designer brand known to man. I don't frequent malls and department stores much, but when I do, I spot a reoccurring scene: designer signs have taken over, and with the signs go higher price tags. Even toddlers are sporting their wares, and they can't even spell!

> Trends are trendy, to say the least. They are constantly changing. That's what they are designed to do.

Don't ask me the last time I saw Aigner. No one knows the woman. In fact, you might be shocked to learn that Etienne Aigner wasn't a woman at all, but a Hungarian-born man who opened his first showroom in New York in 1959. I never met Etienne. He never heard of me; yet he acquired some of my hard-earned cash.[17]

How many designers have you met? Better yet, how many have met you, or *your* hard-earned cash? Have you ever dined with them or been invited to their abode? Do their names cross your mind each time you lug their ten-pound purse down the street, or move it from one end of the counter to the other? Were you or your kin included in any of their wills? Ladies and gentlemen, take a seat. We need to have a serious talk about the contents in our closets. Trends are trendy, to say the least. They are constantly changing. That's what they're designed to do. I used to hear my mother talk about styles that were returning after 40 years. Everything she said had a 40-year timeline! Hats, coats, dresses, shoes! Who would have guessed that Mama would be right? Skirt lengths have gone up, then down, then to the knee, and now they're everywhere in-between. Movies from the 50's parade dresses with three-quarter length sleeves. Energetic *American Bandstand* girls from the 60's twisted and turned in sleeveless shifts. Today, you'd be hard pressed to find a dress in any style other than these. Even seersucker has resurfaced. On our feet we wear everything from vintage soles to flats, made popular in the 60's, when Annette and Frankie wiggled to beach tunes. A recent internet search revealed 519 selections on one site *alone* of the modern-day high heel, coined, a stiletto. (Are they called that because they resemble stilts? Just a thought.)

Why do we have to keep buying and buying and buying? Why do we feel as if we need as many changes of clothing as a backstage runway model? Who can even remember what's in their closet, or under the bed, or both? I remember years ago helping a dear friend pack up her wardrobe as she and her family prepared for a move. She had to tend to matters in the kitchen, so she left me alone in her bedroom. Being the queen of frugality, she knows how to find a bargain, but bargains can even get out of hand. As I fetched a mountain of flats and pumps from the back of her closet, between the night stands, and underneath the bed, I began to see a pattern forming, and couldn't resist the humor of it all. I left her a cute little sticky note which we still laugh about today: "How many pairs of black shoes does a black woman need?"

If you recruited someone to pack up your bedroom, what note would they leave? Would they poke fun at your abundance of black shoes? That's a popular color these days. How about belts, scarves, and vests? After all, a woman's gotta have accessories, right? What about you men? Do you own suits, ties, and handkerchiefs for every day of the week? Since Corporate America has gone casual on Fridays, do you possess a row of nicely starched khakis and sweaters? Let's not forget about the array of athletic wear. After all, everything has to match when you're on the court or the greens. It makes or breaks your game, right? Wrong. Neither the tennis ball nor the golf ball makes it to its destination because an embroidered emblem rests on your sleeve. Your favorite tennis and golf celebrities probably get much of their clothing gifted to them, and a whole lot more. Your special gift comes in the form of a credit card bill!

Can we shake ourselves and begin to emulate just a few habits of a minimalist? Yes, the cliché says that *more is better*, but how does the accumulation of material things affect your financial bottom-line? Unless you have a million-dollar endorsement headed your way, the bottom *will* continue to fall out of your portfolio, and there won't be anything left for the rainy day; and the sound of thunder is closer than we want to admit.

The clothing tips in this chapter may be right up your alley or so far-fetched that you can't see yourself doing them. That's okay. Just find what works for you; find a lot of what works for you; just get rolling. And remember, someone might be ready to leave *you* a sticky note!

COSMETICS and TOILETRIES

$ _____ Use 1" less floss in the morning.

$ _____ Use 1" less floss in the evening.

$ _____ Use ¼ less toothpaste.

$ _____ Use ¼ less mouthwash.

$ _____ Add water to your shampoo. (Why not? Don't the manufacturers? Read their labels.)

$ _____ Add water to your conditioner.

$ _____ Use witch hazel as a skin toner.

$ _____ Add water to your facial moisturizer.

$ _____ Use less hair spray, spritzer, and oil sheen.

$ _____ Touch up your own gray roots.

$ _____ Use a raw egg in warm water for a deep hair conditioner. It contains biotin. (I didn't know as a child how much of a chemist my Mom was!)

$ _____ Identify the toiletry item which you waste the most. Transfer it into a small container.

$ _____ Use half mouthwash and half hydrogen peroxide as an oral rinse. (It's a tip straight from my brother, the dentist.)

$ _____ Use olive oil for a hair hot oil treatment.

$ _____ Stretch each hair dyeing appointment by an extra week.

$ _____ Skip name brand mouthwash.

$ _____ Skip name brand floss; a string is a string.

$ _____ Use one less perfume squirt.

$ _____ Use one less after shave squirt.

$ _____ Buy a combination shampoo and conditioner.

$ _____ Use a pump hair spray. We tend to pump less than spray!

$ _____ Use a bar of soap until the bar breaks. Then press it back together and go a few more days.

$ _____ Have your hair done at a beauty school.

$ _____ Use a facial cleansing bar instead of liquid. It should last longer.

$ _____ Soothing bath crystals are no more than glorified magnesium sulfate salt. Add your own fragrance & soak away.

$ _____ Avoid using products with pre-measured pump-dispensed containers; switch to containers where *you* determine what little amount to dispense.

$ _____ Women, skip perfume for one week.

$ _____ Men, skip cologne for one week.

$ _____ Stock up on regularly used essential toiletries when on sale for "2 for 1."

$ _____ Buy one box of store brand facial tissues.

$ _____ Buy one store brand deodorant.

$ _____ Get your massage from the local massage school.

$ _____ Skip the monthly manicure and pull out an emery board.

$ _____ Still using too much mouthwash? Use a dropper.

$ _____ Do your own nails.

$ _____ Use a disposable razor two extra days than usual before discarding.

$ _____ Buy cologne vs. perfume. It's generally less expensive.

$ _____ Buy perfume lotion vs. perfume.

$ _____ Pluck your own facial hairs! **Ouch!**

$ _____ Women, do your own eyebrow wax job! **Ouch again!**

$ _____ Men, do your own moustache trim.

$ _____ Dig out the last part of the lipstick with a lip brush.

$ _____ Ladies, when eating, remove food from eating utensils with your teeth, not your lips to extend the length of time for the lipstick.

$ _____ Drink liquids with a straw to preserve your lipstick.

$ _____ Put lipstick on one lip and press lips together! (Don't tell my beauty consultant friend Robin that I said this! She said this is a no-no; in this case, I say it's a yes-yes!)

$ _____ Use store brand cosmetics.

$ _____ Buy cheap lipstick to wear before meals and regular lipstick for afterwards.

$ _____ Buy 24-hour lasting lipstick. (My husband reminded me of this product. How would I ever think of this; it's more expensive!)

$ _____ Don't wear any of these products if you plan to stay at home all day; but do brush your teeth!

$ _____ Your Idea – _____.

$ _____ Your Idea – _____.

$ _____ Your Idea – _____.

$ _____ TOTAL ANNUAL SAVINGS

CLOTHING and ACCESSORIES

$ _____   Put taps on the heels of a pair of shoes. You can do it!

$ _____   Borrow an outfit. I once borrowed a mink jacket to attend a function with my husband. No one was more surprised than I was a year later, when my friend *gave me* the jacket! She said she no longer wore it and felt that I would probably be attending many functions with my husband, that would call for nice attire. Wow!

$ _____   Wait to receive your favorite store's coupon before making your next clothing purchase. They *always* have sales.

$ _____   Buy a reversible coat.

$ _____   Buy a reversible belt.

$ _____   Buy a reversible hat.

$ _____   Place one of your designer items on consignment.

$ _____   Buy gloves and scarves at the end of the winter season.

$ _____   Buy boots at the end of the winter season.

$ _____   Buy gold plated earrings. No one gets close enough to know the difference.

$ _____   Buy a gold-plated necklace.

$ _____   In the market for a diamond? Buy a cubic zirconia or a crystal instead; just once.

$ _____   Do you eat in your car? Protect your clothes with a piece of plastic to reduce your dry-cleaning bill.

$ _____   Dry clean on "special days."

$ _____   Use a dry cleaner that offers special rates for multiple items.

$ _____   Hand wash a dry cleanable item that is also washable.

$ _____   Use clear polish to stop pantyhose runs.

$ _____   Buy washables clothes vs. dry cleanable.

$ _____   Buy the next dry cleanable piece of clothing from a consignment store.

$ _____   Buy the next dry cleanable piece of clothing from a thrift store.

$ _____   Skip the Easter outfit.

$ _____   Wear the same pair of earrings or cufflinks for a year.

$ _____   Have a color analysis done. I learned years ago why *cool* colors made me look lifeless, and sterling silver jewelry was less than sterling on me. *Warm* colors are my forte'.

$ _____   Buy one less pair of shoes.

$ _____   Don't buy new shoes; buy shoe polish.

$ _____   Forego shoes with odd colors; stick to the basics.

$ _____   Your Idea - _____.

$ _____   Your Idea - _____.

$ _____   Your Idea - _____.

$ _____   TOTAL ANNUAL SAVINGS

> I never heard of a fashion designer picking up the tab for a destitute nursing home resident. Quit paying for their future indulgences.

· SEVEN ·

Financials: *From Piddly to Prosperous*

"Save something every month, even if you can't afford it." What an odd statement coming from someone who had just spent hours advising us to live within our means. It seemed oxymoronic and impossible. I was living paycheck to paycheck; nevertheless, I took him at his word. Better yet, I took him at his testimony.

I had never met the man before that day. Tom Fortson was an unassuming gentleman with a kind smile. He was a dear friend of a dear friend. His resumé trumpeted his accomplishments: a high-ranking administrator at General Motors (GM®) and Vice President of Human Resources at Atlanta-based Edwards Baking Company, to name a few. Either one of these positions would have been highly esteemed by anyone, especially an African-American male. But it wasn't Tom's resumé that attracted me, nor was it his authoritative, yet mild-mannered presentation. It was the fact that he had walked away from a six-figure income and Corporate America status to pursue full-time Christian ministry. His life validated that material things took a backseat to eternal things. Yes, Tom had the floor. He had something of value to say, and he had my undivided attention.

It was October of 1984. It had only been a little over a year since I had taken a job that paid less than the previous one. Therapy jobs in the early 80's were next to slim and none, so I took a school-based position when it was offered to me. A stint of unemployment coupled with part-time work had preceded this period. While my salary had dropped, the bills hadn't. Rent, utilities, and car expenses stayed the course, along with furniture payments and everything else to which I was committed. Fortunately, I had managed to make it out of college with that one credit card *gift* presented to me during my junior year. I don't remember maxing it out in college,

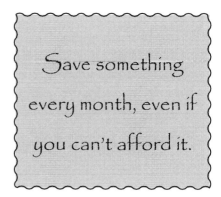

Save something every month, even if you can't afford it.

but a history of slow and inconsistent monthly payments followed me from Virginia to Georgia. Despite having landed a *real* job by that time, I could only get approval for a major credit card that required total payoff each month. That actually turned out to be a temporary "blessing" (for lack of a better word), because I was forced to pay it off each month. I had to learn some sense of restraint early in my working career, no matter how attractive the Sunday newspaper advertisements looked.

So, there I sat on a Saturday morning at my new church home, listening to a tall, soft-spoken man unfold the truths of stewardship in a manner I had never heard. The salary that I received every month, the payroll check that I cashed and put in my bank, did not belong to me. It never did and it never would. I was just a steward, commissioned by God to handle *His* funds. I was to be accountable and intentional with every dollar spent. I was to be generous in my giving towards Kingdom work. I represented the Lord in how I paid my bills, and I was to save for the future. Throughout the morning, Tom repeatedly hammered the point: "It doesn't belong to you… it doesn't belong to you… it doesn't."

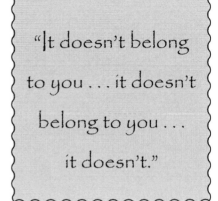

"It doesn't belong to you . . . it doesn't belong to you . . . it doesn't."

We broke for lunch, prepared by sweet church ladies who knew how to make a meal talk! We huddled in small groups, recounting the morning's presentation and suggesting how it might look in our situations. Singles, married couples, and widows alike were poised for the afternoon session and eager to know what the secret was in clearing the financial hurdles in our lives. Tom passed out a simple one-page budget form. It started with the priority he had highlighted all morning. We were stewards. Stewards are intentional, orderly, and responsible. They manage the property of another. But Christian stewards are more than that. They are *thankful* stewards who express their gratitude in tangible ways. The first is in their generous giving. So that was at the top of the list. Some call it *freewill giving* while others refer to it as *tithing*. Whatever the case, it was first on the list.

That paper was powerful! It changed my life. It prodded me to shift from a focus on myself to a focus on becoming a generous giver. But how could I do that? The numbers didn't lie. When I subtracted the household bills, credit obligations, a little food and water, and an occasional night of entertainment, the leftovers were piddly. And so was my generosity. (Talk about an oxymoron!)

Save something every month, even if you can't afford it. Those words rang in my ears as I filled in the numbers. The monthly income balance inched closer to zero with each entry. *Save something.* The utilities were unchangeable. *Save something.* I have to buy gas, groceries, and deodorant! *Save something.* I wrote in my piddly "giving" amount. How shameful. How pathetic, given the bounty lavished upon me over the years. It made no sense to deceive myself by entering a larger amount. My spirit churned from within. This number, by God's grace, would change. It would change drastically. But how? Numbers don't lie.

Tom poked fun at the budget exercise as we worked our way through the categories. When he covered utility costs, in particular the phone, he told husbands that it was cheaper to fly his wife home to visit her mom each month than it was for them to talk on the phone. The chuckling male attendees got the message. Long-distance calls back then came with an outrageous price. It was cheaper to talk in person than to have your hard-earned dollars slip away on Ma Bell's utility poles. Nevertheless, the phone calls were a permissible entry. Later on, Tom received a round of applause when he admonished men to let their wives write in their weekly hair appointment entries. I recall the men shaking their heads but yielding to the mandate.

Every single and couple combed their way through the form, vowing to finish the task. No skipping of lines. No skirting the obvious. Light chatter and occasional chuckles helped to alleviate the uneasiness that provoked squirming in our seats. Each person had his own challenges, his own wasteful areas, and his own resolve.

We finally reached the personification of Tom's oxymoronic statement. The *Savings* category. Save something every month, even if you can't afford it. There it was again. The impossible was staring me in the face. Did I believe the morning's message? Was I truly a steward over God's generous resources? Did I trust that He would transform my budget, meet my needs, and be as faithful in my life as He had obviously been in Tom's? I stared at the line. *Savings*. I glanced at the remaining categories yet to be filled in. I shifted in my seat, knowing that the remaining income balance was quickly headed from the black to the red. *Save something*. I took a deep breath, gripped my pencil ever so tightly, and wrote in $25. That amount over the course of a year wouldn't amount to much, but it would be the start of a new financial modus operandi that has continued to unfold and be fine-tuned decades later.

Each person's financial situation is different. There are parts we can't control. There are probably greater parts that we can. Time is too short, and you have too much to accomplish for me to summarize all the details of *my* "save something" saga. I will tell you that in less than 15 months I was debt free! If a single woman on a "fixed income" with monthly obligations can make a complete financial turnaround, so can you. You just have to be willing to face the music, make the hard decisions, and work the plan.

> A meager $25 can birth a desire to transform your saving, giving, and spending.

Many of us are at a crossroads: we can wine and dine ourselves along life's journey, only to end up in substandard care, or we can purpose to gain control of our spending *now* and have more options in our twilight years. And those years are closer than we'd like to admit. There's no doubt that we all have been jerked around by self-induced financial slip-ups or seductive lures from slick marketing campaigns. Don't despair. Today, you have regained your place in the driver's seat! Hold on as you maneuver the twists and turns towards financial success, keeping in mind that new and improved wise decisions are at the helm. Things may get tight along the way, but remember the words of Tom Fortson: *Save something every month, even if you can't afford it.*

SAVINGS FOR THE PIDDLY

$ _____ Adjust exemptions to decrease your tax refund and increase your monthly take-home pay (to accelerate debt-busting and propel investing.)

$ _____ Donate stuff to reduce taxes.

$ _____ Do the calculations to determine if itemizing your taxes vs. using the standard deduction is more profitable.

$ _____ It seems more favorable to do consistent monthly investing (for dollar-cost averaging benefits) versus sporadic investing.

$ _____ Make investment deposits automatic from bank/credit union accounts to financial institutions to guarantee consistent investing.

$ _____ Determine (with the help of a reputable financial advisor schooled in insurance) the most affordable, but beneficial, life insurance product for your **long-term** needs.

$ _____ Don't buy any financial product that you don't understand and can't explain to someone else! (Remember my story and Appendix A entries!)

$ _____ Dispute credit card errors and other bill discrepancies in writing.

$ _____ Don't pay for a credit report. They are free once per year per credit bureau. Order a free copy from one of the three every four months to cover the entire year.

$ _____ Adjust state exemptions to avoid receiving a refund; you'll only have to declare it as income and pay tax on it the next year.

$ _____ Decline all credit card offers.

$ _____ Cut up cards when they arrive.

$ _____ Barter with a friend.

$ _____ Invest your salary raise the first month received. Don't get accustomed to the additional income.

$ _____ Keep a log for one month of every *penny* spent.

$ _____ Read *Rich Dad Poor Dad* [17] for a fresh perspective on owning a business versus just having a job.

$ _____   Avoid purchasing insurance for things already covered by other means.

$ _____   Use Turbo Tax® or another tax software program to maximize all allowable tax write- offs.

$ _____   Pay extra on credit card balances to eliminate the debt faster.

$ _____   Carry envelopes with budgeted cash amounts for categories most tempting in terms of excess spending. For many of us, these categories may include *Eating Out, Groceries, Entertainment,* and *Miscellaneous.*

$ _____   Don't use payday loan places ever. I hear that their interest rates over the length of the loan can run in the hundreds!

$ _____   Don't buy any of that stuff that's advertised in credit card bills.

$ _____   Avoid using those "credits" that are attached to credit card points. You'll end up charging even *more* stuff!

$ _____   Ask a wealthy person for a tip on saving.

$ _____   For a checking account, find a money market account that offers a higher interest rate than regular checking accounts.

$ _____   Double check credit card bills for errors (and downright lies).

$ _____   Join a credit union – less fees.

$ _____   Switch credit card debt to a 0% credit card that you can pay off the month **before** the 0% expires, and pay it off like your hair's on fire! Be sure to pay the bill electronically each month as *soon* as the bill arrives to avoid forfeiting the 0%. If you are late even one time, you could be charged the higher exorbitant rate until the remaining balance is paid off!

$ _____   Bundle car and home insurance.

$ _____   Pay cash vs. writing checks or even using a debit card.

$ _____   Pay cash vs. charging. That'll save you a bundle!

$ _____   Do online banking to reduce the number of stamps used.

$ _____   Do online banking to reduce the number of checks written.

$ _____   Switch to credit cards with no annual fee.

$ _____   Avoid ATM surcharges.

$ _____   Pay bills on time to avoid late fees.

$ _____   Have your payroll check directly deposited to avoid a monthly bank/credit maintenance fee.

$ _____   Collect loose change in your pocket.

$ _____   Collect loose change in your car.

$ _____   Write out your debts! That'll shake you up!

$ _____   Ask for credit card interest rate reductions. All they can say is no. Call them each month to make a request.

$ _____   Have any tax refund checks directly deposited into a Roth IRA account.

$ _____   Roll your own coins in wrappers; don't pay 4% to a bank or a machine to do that!

$ _____   Total the amount of finance charges paid last year on credit cards! (That'll be an eye-opener.)

$ _____   Total the amount of finance charges paid last year on your car loan!

$ _____   Total the amount of finance charges paid last year on your mortgage! (Talk about a million-dollar loss!)

$ _____   Order standard checks vs. signature or designer checks.

$ _____   Young people: just save your raises for the next 10 years.

$ _____   Got a pocket full of debt monsters? Cut up one each month.

$ _____   Your Idea - _____.

$ _____   Your Idea - _____.

$ _____   Your Idea - _____.

$ _____   TOTAL ANNUAL SAVINGS

· EIGHT ·

House Savings: *There Went the Million*

I hate snakes. I hate the plastic ones dangling from dollar store hooks. I hate the glossy photos in the *National Geographic*. I hate public television's documentaries on every rare species on the planet. My disdain for these pole-shaped creatures goes all the way back to childhood. From the one that slithered across my path the afternoon I descended the school bus steps, to the intruder that took advantage of an open window and meandered his way up the stairs before my brother discovered it, to the trio hanging out on our family's porch, disrupting our serene Sunday afternoon.

I hate snakes. Their presence can go unnoticed until they're so close that you hurt yourself trying to get away from them. Their bite can make you sick, and they can squeeze the life out of you. Mortgages are like snakes. Their impact can go unnoticed, especially if you close on your mortgage towards the end of the month and the first payment doesn't come due until two months later. The payments can make you sick. They can squeeze the life out of any budget. And you can hurt yourself trying to get away from them.

As a single woman, I worked full time most years, but managed to pursue real estate on the side (just like my Dad.) My license made me privy to viewing homes on a whim, which accelerated my own home purchase. How convenient to be the buyer *and* the salesperson at the closing. Imagine, earning a commission for buying your own home! Anyway, as a new homeowner, I began making timely payments and sometimes paying extra on the principal. This was a concept espoused by consumer advocates and Christian financial personalities within an earshot of my radio. Paying extra on occasion may have felt like a step in the right direction, but it didn't make a huge dent in the amortization schedule.

Windfalls, Weddings, and Weary Moves

In the early 2000's when our family was emotionally mending from Mom's sudden death, the economic climate in this country was making a rebound, and mortgage rates were beginning to drop. I called my Dad one day for his advice on whether I should refinance my mortgage balance for a lower rate. His response was unexpected and in the form of a question: "How much do you owe on your house and car?" A few weeks later, I was not refinancing, I was paying off my house *and* car. And what was the source of that unexpected gift? Remember the brown sack in the closet? Mom's generosity had struck again, posthumously. Dad had sent his little girl a hefty little money order, and she was (once again) debt-free!

Several years passed, and despite this joyous financial windfall, I had a gut-level unsettling that my salary had not been adjusted downward when my weekly work hours had been reduced. I wasn't living paycheck-to-paycheck, and my contracted work-week caused my salary to fluctuate month-to-month, so I wasn't quite sure how much I was bringing home. I brought this issue to the attention of the human resources department, and after a brief time of research, my feelings were confirmed in a conciliatory letter, and I was presented with a repayment plan for a sizeable amount. This news hit around the same time that Dad experienced his health crisis. Weighing the circumstances, Dad's needs came first, followed by the repayment plan. This meant that my recently declared snowball savings efforts would have to be shifted to the back burner. After all, in my opinion, I had *burned* through precious fortunes and drifted from debt-free world twice already! My needs had to take second place to Dad's care.

> Regardless of our carefully crafted life plans, we never know what is around the corner.

Regardless of our carefully crafted life plans, we never know what's around the corner, do we? Life happens when it happens. For me, it involved wedding bells! After waiting half-a-century plus one year, I walked the aisle of a packed church, draped in a stunning ivory, beaded, halter-style gown that hugged my silhouette, causing my husband-to-be to light up like the Macy's Christmas tree. Overnight, our housing options doubled. We both had homes, but decided to make my domicile our primary living quarters. Anthony's home, occupied by a family member, would be our getaway spot when we needed to retreat from the daily grind. This routine continued for a year until the sudden announcement that the home would be vacated within two months. The news sent this blissful bride's brain into project manager attack mode. I knew that we needed to draft a plan and implement it quickly.

Anthony and I sought advice from reputable realtors regarding the housing market's climate (which had tanked by this time.) Taking into account the huge loss we would incur if we sold it, we sat down for a late-night pow-wow to objectively weigh all the options. Do we live here? Do we live there? Should we sell? Should we rent? Which do we rent, one or both? And for how long? We hammered away at all the scenarios, laying out the pros and cons of each. By the time we finished, I had drafted the most colorful spreadsheet known to man. The decision was clear-cut, sensible, and mutually agreed upon. We would remain where we were and rent out Anthony's house.

Well, as stupid would have it, we began listening to voices. Not voices in our heads, but those from well-intentioned friends suggesting that we dump both houses and buy a place of our own as newlyweds. We had weighed that option, but it didn't seem wise at the time. But what happened next is still an absolute

our grave! Just the sight of that would have sent me to my grave! The struggle was so fierce tha   he neighbors heard the ruckus. I know it must have been traumatic, to say the least. I'm sure he must have reached his limit with these dirt-eating monsters. But what possessed him to snap pictures and prir t out an 8 x 10 glossy of the defeated foe, and present it over my left shoulder while I sat calmly on the sofa? He *knows* I don't like glossy shots. *You* know I don't like glossy shots. God knows how much I can bear!

Now, I'm not so naive as to think that we can completely eliminate home expenses. Whether we r nt or buy, expenses are inevitable. And renting has its own set of challenges, like Richard with the sh tgun, and the creep in the laundry room. (That's another book in another genre.)

As you probably already guessed, I grew up with very frugal parents. Many of their habits have abbed off on me. I know the benefit of saying no. If we're honest with ourselves, we know that we do 't need to lug home every new gadget at the local home improvement store just because the man in th rightly colored apron says it will make our lives easier. The very thing that you think you *must* have r y just be closer than you think. It may be collecting dust in your neighbor's garage! All it takes is a sim e request to borrow it.

Next to the bedroom, we Americans spend a great deal of our day in the kitchen. Whether searching for a cold beverage, zapping dinner in the microwave, dipping the last scoop of sherbet, or hunting for another midnight snack, we love our kitchens. While our waistlines are expanding, our pocketbooks are dwindling due to excess waste. Choosing to make a few small changes can add a wealth of savings to our pocketbooks; wouldn't you agree? So, let's turn off the TV, silence all electronic devices, open the attic, basement, and closet doors, and see how many wasted dollars you can uncover right under your roof. And pray that you don't uncover anything moving in the basement.

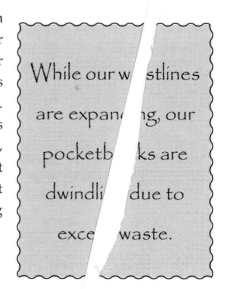

While our w stlines are expan ng, our pocketb ks are dwindli due to exce waste.

BATHROOM SAVINGS

$ _____   Don't run water while brushing your teeth.

$ _____   Don't run water while washing your face.

$ _____   Cut showering time by one minute.

$ _____   Only use the exhaust fan when actually in the shower.

$ _____   Don't run water until ready to jump into the shower.

$ _____   Capture rain water to rinse your car and water plants.

$ _____   Use one inch less bath water in the bathtub.

$ _____   Put a brick in the toilet tank to raise the water line and decrease the amount of water needed to flush.

$ _____   Keep hair out of the sink.

$ _____   Use a low-water showerhead.

$ _____   No bleach tabs in the toilet tank. (A plumber told me that they eat away at the rubber seals.)

$ _____   Use two less pieces of toilet paper.

$ _____   Separate your two-ply toilet paper. (Okay, okay; I won't get mad if you skip this one!)

$ _____   Take wet slithers of soap and press them all together.

$ _____   No singing in the shower. It wastes water!

$ _____   Take slightly cooler showers.

$ _____   Take slightly cooler baths.

$ _____   No exhaust fan with quick shower.

$ _____   Have a light fixture with smaller bulb wattage.

$ _____   If you live alone, use a space heater/small fan once per month versus the house AC/heating system.

$ _____   Turn off a space heater immediately after getting out of the shower.

$ _____   Your Idea _____.

$ _____   Your Idea _____.

KITCHEN SAVINGS

$ _____ Put a cookie jar in the kitchen for collecting loose change (and dollars.)

$ _____ Use a hand towel vs. paper towels to dry hands.

$ _____ Use half a paper towel.

$ _____ Add water to dish detergent.

$ _____ Squirt ¼ less dishwashing liquid in the sink.

$ _____ Pour ¼ less dishwasher detergent in the machine.

$ _____ Use the smallest size storage bags possible.

$ _____ Use the smallest size freezer bags possible.

$ _____ Use flip-lock sandwich bags vs. more expensive zip-style.

$ _____ Use select-a-size paper towels.

$ _____ Use the smaller burner on the stove.

$ _____ Turn the stove off one minute before suggested cooking time; the burner is still hot, and so is the skillet.

$ _____ Save reusable pieces of aluminum foil.

$ _____ Use ¼ less foil.

$ _____ Use ¼ less plastic wrap.

$ _____ Use toaster oven versus the stove's oven for quickly cooked items.

$ _____ Buy store brand paper towels.

$ _____ Buy store brand dinner napkins.

$ _____ Cover food in the microwave with a microwave lid vs. using paper towels.

$ _____ Use half of a steel wool pad.

$ _____ Try not to open the freezer until ready to put in two or more items (Combining those trips could potentially keep the freezer's temperature constant, avoiding the use of more electricity.)

$ _____ Try not to open the refrigerator until ready to put in two or more items. (Same concept as above.)

Snowball Investing

$ _____   Try not to open the freezer until ready to take out two or more items.

$ _____   Try not to open the refrigerator until ready to take out two or more items.

$ _____   Set the oven on broil to preheat the oven faster. (My Mom taught me this!)

$ _____   Heat food a few seconds less in the microwave.

$ _____   Keep grease out of the kitchen sink to avoid the need for a plumber.

$ _____   Use a manual can opener.

$ _____   Buy stainless steel skillets; non-stick ones wear out too quickly!

$ _____   Just once, buy the cheapest foil.

$ _____   Handwash dishes.

$ _____   Fill the sink only with the amount of water needed to cover the dishes.

$ _____   Turn the oven off two minutes before scheduled time if you know the food will be totally cooked.

$ _____   Use the stove vent for minimum time and on the lowest speed.

$ _____   Cook more than one food item in the oven at the same time.

$ _____   Your Idea - _____.

$ _____   Your Idea - _____.

$ _____   Your Idea - _____.

OTHER ROOMS

$ _____ Use ¼ less scoop of clothes detergent.

$ _____ Fresh flowers – change water often and cut stems to prolong their life.

$ _____ Use half of a dryer sheet.

$ _____ Reuse dryer sheets.

$ _____ Use a water filter pitcher instead of bottled water.

$ _____ Bundle home repairs – A prospective home contractor charged $80 for providing bathroom renovation and gutter replacement estimates. I asked him to clean the gutters while he was on the roof!

$ _____ Put one household item on consignment.

$ _____ Shop home insurance annually.

$ _____ Condense trash to save bags: put cups/cans inside one another; cut up take home containers.

$ _____ Use carpet runners/rugs in high traffic areas to reduce the number of carpet-cleaning services.

$ _____ Fix faucet leaks.

$ _____ Buy seasonal appliances (fans/heaters) at the end of the season.

$ _____ Collect aluminum cans to recycle or sell.

$ _____ Collect glass to recycle or sell.

$ _____ Unscrew flashlights to save battery life.

$ _____ Attend free "how to" clinics.

$ _____ Line trashcans with plastic bags.

$ _____ Increase your home insurance deductible.

$ _____ Hang a few clothes in the sun to dry. (But don't get thrown out of your subdivision for violating homeowners' association rules!)

$ _____ If you use timed air fresheners, take batteries out often to extend their life.

$ _____ Steam clean your own carpet.

$ _____ Don't rent furniture or electronics.

$ _____ Down comforter – keep it extra clean by putting it inside a duvet cover or between two sheets like they do at the hotel.

$ _____ Consult a friend/coworker regarding house problems. (My contractor friend Walter told me that inserting the end of a broom handle in the drain and twisting it would fix my "locked-up" garbage disposal problem. I did what he said and the disposal worked like a charm!)

$ _____ Do one home repair yourself!

$ _____ Install smoke detectors to lower homeowners' insurance cost.

$ _____ Make your own window treatments.

$ _____ Make sure new appliance upgrades qualify for available tax energy rebates.

$ _____ Your Idea - _____.

$ _____ Your Idea - _____.

$ _____ Your Idea - _____.

$ _____ TOTAL ANNUAL SAVINGS

A 15-year mortgage can save you thousands! Contact your mortgage lender today to find out the refinancing costs.

· NINE ·

Kids, Pets, and Pregnancy: *Margaret, Megan, and Me*

Let's face it: pregnancy costs money, kids cost even more money, and most pets will eat you out of house and home. Before babies are ever born, they have a pristine nursery awaiting their arrival. Never mind that they'll sleep most of the day and aren't even able to see or touch the nursery theme characters mounted on the walls and dangling in their cribs. And when they do decide to peer through those baby blues, they can only see your masterfully color-coordinated décor in black and white! So, who is the nursery design *really* for?

Frankly speaking, I can't relate to the daily ordeal of curbing expenses in the areas of pets, pregnancy, and kids. I've never been pregnant, I don't have biological children, and the only pets I've personally been responsible for are my three stuffed dogs Fred, Freda, and Marvin. So, pardon me while I borrow from a lifetime of observations, as well as a gazillion stories from a gazillion friends who have had a gazillion children (averaging four to seven per family.) They know the thrill of victorious saving and the agony of financial depletion. Despite the size of their families, the kids were clothed, fed, educated (even while one pregnant mom was homeschooling on bedrest), highly-educated, and now (for the majority) living on their own. (Parents are so grateful for the bliss of empty-nesting.)

While moms and dads struggle to shore up an iron-clad defense against little Johnny's pleas for everything on Saturday morning commercials, getting a grasp on the tactics of marketing is like holding jelly. Just when you think you've gotten a handle on it, something slips through and makes a big mess. And the subtlety of marketing is at work in the most unlikely place: schools. You send your children off on that big yellow bus, or inch your way through the drop-off lane, not realizing the magnitude of what awaits them: the school of marketing. So, parents, grab your bookbag and get ready to join your kids on the b-u-s. Endure the bouncy seats on the five back rows. Brace yourself as you come to a screeching halt in front of the widely-stretched brick building. Watch your step as you descend those steep stairs. Good morning everyone. Let's walk through the corridors and take a peek at commercialism in action.

> The subtlety of marketing is at work in the most unlikely place: schools.

You have purchased quality sneakers for your child or grandchild, only theirs don't have a celebrity's name embedded on the side. As the little ones shuffle their way towards homeroom, they pass gobs of peers sporting hooked logos on the side of their sneakers. Your child comes home whining for the *hook*. You explain to them how comfortable their shoes are, and they are appeased for a night. As soon as the next day's bell rings and the trek towards homeroom begins again, those *hooks* are staring them in the face. To rub salt into the wound, the added *"bling, bling"* light-up shoes intensify the differences. And the comparisons go on and on, from head to toe.

Get the students settled into their desks and the fun really begins. Picture day is coming! Everyone's highly encouraged to buy the whole package. The class with 100% participation gets a free picture in each package, plus a pizza party! So, not only does Johnny not have *hooked* or *glowing* shoes, he now has two more hurdles to overcome: the Friday morning spelling test and the pressure of begging Mom and Dad for picture money; money that he overheard them say last night "is just not there."

Let the school year get underway and the Labor Day holiday pass. Now comes the cafeteria assembly. The high-tech video rolls out the school-wide fundraiser. An army of potential prizes are paraded before the students' gleaming eyes. If they sell $50 of goods, they receive a $10 gift reward! Sell more and the rewards keep rising! The prizes start small with neon-colored pencils and light-up erasers, and mushroom into such an array of electronic devices that only the super strong-willed child can resist. You know I'm telling the truth. I know you're nodding your head or shaking it under the weight of guilt! So off little Johnny goes with his tri-fold glossy brochure, eager to make the most sales in the class in order to win the BIG prize. It's legitimate; after all, we live in a free-enterprise society. It's not even infringing upon antiquated child labor laws, is it?

Need I bore you with the costs of raffles, soccer uniforms, and cheerleader pom-poms; and many of these are for kindergarteners!! Lord, help the parents! They can't save for Johnny's college because he's got to make the little league team and travel across the southeast. Never mind that he can't spell most of the states through which he'll be traveling! Readers, remember the title of this book. Self-defeating decisions are melting snowflakes all around us, resulting in financial ruin with each head-turning attraction.

Here's a quick history lesson for millennials. Ever heard of the yellow pages? They were the world's format for business advertising. They came into existence in America in the late 1880s when a newspaper printer in Wyoming ran out of white paper and decided to use the available color, which just happened to be yellow. The concept later expanded to include advertisement of businesses in regions throughout the world.[19] If you happen to stumble upon a volume of this book, take a quick glance. Most listings are a conglomeration of alphabetically arranged names, addresses, and phone numbers. Some contain pictures of companies' logos. Sprinkled throughout the book are various-sized ads in boxes. They may appear to be randomly located, but someone told me a long time ago that the most expensive section for advertising on a page is the top right quadrant. That's the place where the eyes first glance as you flip the pages.

We all know that yellow pages are sparse these days. I miss them. I miss their size, their color, and their weight. They were quite versatile for many uses besides finding businesses. You could hold a door open with them. They were a makeshift booster seat for a toddler. You could even toss one across the room when you needed to let off some steam! (No, I never did that!)

Realistically speaking, the yellow pages haven't left us. In fact, we have more yellow pages now than ever before. We just don't recognize them as such because most are not yellow. These "pages" eruptively appear in the margins of our computer screen. They invade our selectively chosen websites in the form of pop-ups, slide-ins, and drop-downs. They interrupt our time of relaxing instrumental music playing. They used to be displayed along interstates in still-life. Now these pages, better known as billboards, are no longer still. They're constantly changing. In fact, they're downright distracting. That's what they're intended to do. They are intended to distract us away from driving and towards the displayed product or service.

Pet owners, you're not immune to the lures of Madison Avenue either. Sign up for one pet store rewards program, and the pet world starts nipping at your wallet from here onward. And you poor pregnant women; register on one baby website and the cookies invade your electronic devices, offering the latest crib-to-twin bed furniture conversions before you ever feel the first twinge of labor pains. And once your sweet bundle of joy sees the light of day, the doctor whacks his tush, and his wails echo throughout the delivery corridor, game is on. His satisfaction with mommy's warm and safe cocoon is quickly replaced with the "I-wants."

Real Wants in Action

Have you ever gotten into a fight with a kid? Seriously. I'm not talking about a verbal exchange where heated words were hurled back and forth. I'm talking about a physical fight. Have you at least ever been "jumped" by a kid? I recall my friend Tamara telling me about a short, but shocking incident that she witnessed years ago. The names are fictitious but the details are real. You may have witnessed a similar altercation in your lifetime. It went something like this:

Margaret, the mom, was shopping one day with her daughter, Megan. My friend Tamara happened to round the corner in the store at the time that the mother-daughter dueling began. While Margaret glanced towards a particular item on display, little Megan's eye caught her own little treasure that had been strategically placed on the shelf at eye level for kids. The verbal exchange commenced:

Megan: "Mommy, I want it."
Margaret: "No honey, you don't need that."
Megan: "But Mommy, I want it."
Margaret: "No honey, you don't need it."

At this point, Megan's voice escalated, prompting my friend to glance in their direction. The little girl's protest continued:

Megan: "But Mommy, I WANT IT!"
Margaret: "No honey, you're not getting it."

We all have a little Megan and Margaret in us.

Little Megan had finally reached the point where she was tired of her verbal pleas falling on deaf ears. She tightened her right leg, swung it backwards, and with all of her might, thrust it forward, planting her foot in the middle of her mother's shin. My observing friend let out a gasp and waited for Megan's mother to deliver a well-deserved disciplinary response. I was horrified when Tamara recounted the scene to me. But what happened next was even more horrific. Margaret knelt down, looked into the eyes of her little angel, and replied, "I didn't know you wanted it that badly." At that point, she succumbed to her toddler's demands, placed the toy in her cart, and proceeded down the aisle. The battle was over. The kid had won.

Should I pause and let you catch your breath? Do you need to put the book down and take a short walk? Do you want to find Megan and escort her to an old-fashioned wood shed? Or better yet, would you rather put Margaret over your knee?

Before you pull out your wooden spoon and go on a manhunt for this dysfunctional pair, let me share a secret with you. We all have a little Megan and Margaret in us. Kids, pets, and babies in utero constantly tug at our heart strings. Kids whine for what they want, while babies do flips in tummies (prompting the purchase of yet another cute baby trinket). Thankfully, dogs just sit and wag their tails until you drop a lump of anything edible on the floor.

"But Mommy, I want." Oh, the power of five syllables, especially in the store aisle where Johnny and Megan have an audience, and they launch headfirst into a performance fit for an Oscar®. They know how to start calmly and slowly turn up the heat, like the proverbial frog in water. They may be the ones turning up the heat, but you're the one getting cooked, financially speaking.

No one likes a scene in public. They are embarrassing, they are uncontrollable, and these days they can easily end up on social media for the world to see. You have to determine how to minimize the scenes in your household. But first, you need to harness the Megan in your own heart. Take it from me, every enticing item is at eye level, and the lure to have them resides deep within us all.

You cannot, I repeat, cannot buy everything that you or your children want. If you do, you will end up mortgaging your house for a Happy Meal®! I'm being a little facetious, but as King Solomon wisely said, it's the little foxes that spoil the vine (Song of Solomon 2:15).

Remember why you purchased this book (or someone gave it to you.) You need money for retirement. You need money for health care. You need a reserve for sick care. And if (God forbid) you need funds to cover assisted living and nursing home costs, you need to have something on the vine from which to pluck!

So, are you ready to unearth the Margarets and Megans in the aisles of your life? They're right around the corner. They're on the nearest shelf. Can't you hear their pleas? "I want." "But I want." "But I want it." Snatch those little foxes before they strip the vine bare. But don't forget to wear your shin guards.

> Have your child take a career interest questionnaire to identify their abilities, skills, and talents and help direct them to the most affordable college or trade school.

KIDS, PETS, and PREGNANCY SAVINGS

$ _____   Shop for cheaper pet shots.

$ _____   Give your own pet a bath.

$ _____   Skip pet grooming one month.

$ _____   Pregnant? Buy clothes bimonthly as you expand.

$ _____   Buy maternity clothes at yard sales and thrift shops.

$ _____   Send an email to friends and coworkers, requesting maternity clothes.

$ _____   Kids' clothes are in abundance at yard sales.

$ _____   Reward your kids for not losing clothes, lunch boxes, etc.

$ _____   Give lots of coins vs. dollars for gifts to younger kids.

$ _____   Check parent chat rooms for giveaways.

$ _____   Buy toys at thrift stores.

$ _____   Buy school supplies on sales tax holiday.

$ _____   Buy school clothes on sales tax holiday.

$ _____   Find free summer recreational programs.

$ _____   Give kids $1 each time they drink water at a restaurant (if the price of soda is higher.)

$ _____   Give kids $1 each week they don't drink any sodas.

$ _____   Ask a friend to babysit and return the favor.

$ _____   Barter for a child-related need.

$ _____   Use cloth diapers at home; toss in the washer/dryer at night; they'll be ready for the next day.

$ _____   Want a pet? Go to the shelter. Want a cheap pet? Get a fish!

$ _____   Don't give pet table food; they'll get sick and end up with a huge vet bill.

$ _____   It's time to tell kids there is NO SANTA CLAUS!

$ _____   Shop at a consignment store.

$ _____   Buy clothes out of season.

$ _____   Accept hand-me-downs.

$ _____   Buy children's books at thrift stores.

$ _____   Negotiate lower in-home or daycare rates in exchange for an extended agreement.

$ _____   Buy kids' shoes in upscale thrift store neighborhoods.

$ _____   Bring healthy pre-packaged snacks to the grocery store; give to kids in the checkout line to distract them from tempting treats on the shelves.

$ _____   Potty train kids EARLY to save $$$ on diapers.

$ _____   Cut the feet out of babies' and toddlers' PJs when they outgrow them to extend the wear time.

$ _____   Give kids a treat if the house electric bill decreases by a certain number of dollars.

$ _____   Give a treat if the house gas bill decreases by a certain number of dollars.

$ _____   Give a treat if the water bill decreases by a certain number of dollars.

$ _____   Ask friends about reduced childcare options.

$ _____   Give your daughters sewing lessons.

$ _____   Shop the cost of braces.

$ _____   Birthday cake – buy a plain cake and decorate it.

$ _____   Make cakes for other kids' parties.

$ _____   Private school? Buy used uniforms

$ _____   Go to grocery store without the kids. That alone should save you a quarter of a million over a lifetime!

$ _____   Does your college kid have a credit card? Pay them cash each month they have a zero balance.

$ _____   Attend free kids' arts/crafts shows; ONLY take enough money for lunch, not for supplies and other tempting purchases.

$ _____   Give your children $1 each time they choose a free entertainment (a park vs. putt putt).

$ _____   Your Idea: _____.

$ _____   Your Idea: _____.

$ _____   TOTAL ANNUAL SAVINGS

· TEN ·

Food: *I'll Have That*

Most of us have been clamoring for something to put in our mouths before we were born. Even ultrasounds have captured the images of babies sucking their thumbs in utero. When they finally do enter the world, their cries can be heard reverberating throughout hospital corridors. Some suggest that it's a protest from leaving their warm maternal environment. I'd like to suggest that they are saying, "I want food!"

It goes without saying. We <u>love</u> to eat in the good old USA, whether it's lobster from Maine, spicy Texas chili, Southern deep-dish peach cobbler, or Chicago pizza. We eat in our gourmet kitchens, our secondhand cars, and our corporate cubicles. We eat when we're happy, sad, and bored. Many of you baby boomers may recall your family or a neighbor having a garden where fresh vegetables were only footsteps away.

The farmer in my Dad prompted him to always have a variety of food sources for his family. He would bring home crates of baby chicks, and I would watch as they grew into adults. Dad and my brothers would gather and wash hatched eggs and deliver them to the local grocer for sale. (You had to be creative in the 60's to keep a roof over your head.) My family enjoyed the fruit of Dad's labor through the sales, but also when the feathered friends became the chosen entrée: fried chicken never tasted so good!

Food on the Table

Growing up, my family always had at least one garden each season. They always seemed to yield a bumper crop. Corn stalks grew tall, tomato plants spread widely, and watermelon vines just took over! I remember the year that we planted a few rows of watermelon. Well, it seemed like a few. Anyway, the melons grew, and grew, and grew. By August, the bounty was so huge that we had cold, delicious slices of that luscious fruit for breakfast, lunch, and dinner. Every friend who dropped by got a melon. The neighbors across the street got melons. I even remember one day seeing an unfamiliar car pull into the driveway. The man behind the wheel was just asking for directions. Dad gave him directions *and* a melon! (I can't make this stuff up!)

When we weren't dropping seeds in holes, pulling weeds, and plucking beans off the poles, we were at the local grocery store. My brothers and I sought out our favorite sugary cereal while Mom spent time squeezing the tomatoes for ripeness. Once our overflowing cart reached the counter, I watched in amazement as the checkout clerk punched in the figures of each item on the cash register in lightning speed, while sliding them towards the bagging boy. It was nice not to have to haul those bags outside. We simply piled into our car, Dad would drive up to the curb, and the bagger would roll the cart outside and neatly place every one of those brown bags in the car trunk. I was exposed to the courtesy of customer service early in life.

The production and distribution of today's food has changed. Most of us can't recall the last time we ate hormone-free chicken. Supersized grapes of all colors fill produce shelves, but lack seeds! I spend more time roving through aisles, searching for fruit that smells like fruit, or smells like anything! The colors are radiant, the plumpness is undeniable, but my nose rarely detects life!

Food. We eat it to survive. We eat it on the go. We eat it by ourselves, next to strangers, and with family and friends. It is a big part of our lives. It's a big part of our budgets. Its lure and the symbolism surrounding it even captivates our young ones. I recently read that one of America's well-known fast-food company's symbol is more recognizable than the Christian cross![20]

Food. Everyone has a funny story centered around it. Mine occurred several years ago when I planned a weekend beach getaway with two friends for a birthday celebration. In preparation for the festivities, I pre-ordered a small birthday cake to take on our trip. Friday night was our time to settle into the carefully selected townhouse on Hilton Head Island and enjoy fresh seafood at a nearby restaurant. Saturday morning and afternoon was a time of leisurely shopping at every type of store imaginable. We started at high-end boutiques and wound up at quaint little thrift stores with bargains galore. That evening was the official birthday celebration at another restaurant with mouth-watering menu items. We stuffed ourselves silly over laughs and serious conversation alike, while the waitress gingerly tended to our every need.

As our feasting was nearing the close, and sensing that the waitress was about to launch into her dessert pitch, I informed my friends that a special dessert awaited our return to the townhouse. That was met with affirmative nods. At that moment our waitress began her verbal unpacking of every sort of scrumptious treat known to man. We politely let her speak, assured that our unified response would be a resounding *No*. She was just about to wrap up her list when the words, "blackberry pie" rolled off her tongue, to which I blurted out, "I'll have that!" Who was more surprised than I? Was it a funny moment? Well, let's just say that our trip was over 10 years ago, and the thought of those three words still produce a snicker.

> If your income were cut by 40% could you cut your food budget accordingly?

If your income were cut by 40%, could you cut your food budget accordingly? Chances are, the answer would be, *no way*. Many retirement checks are a meager 60% of a person's regular salary. So how can we retain our eating lifestyle after retirement on less dollars? Simple; cut our eating budget now. If 40% is too much, can you save a dollar or two here and there? Surely you can! We need to tell ourselves **no** before we get to the drive-through window, scan the menu marquee in the fast food line, or open that elegant bi-fold entrée list at the five-star restaurant. Sometimes we need to say **no** before we leave the house. Sometimes we just need to stay home.

Temptation is everywhere, even under your own roof. While I was typing this section in the book, my hubby politely asked me what lunch "looked like" today. I suggested we eat the salad with deli meat in the refrigerator. He suggested take-out at the local Chinese buffet restaurant. I reluctantly agreed, adding the suggestion that we split a meal. As usual, one meal was more than enough, only costing us $9.25. Being the penny pincher that I am, I did a quick calculation to determine the value, if the cost of that one meal had been invested over 20 years at 10%. Guess what? Our spur-of-the-moment lunch would have been worth $7024.16. Chinese food is good, but it ain't *that* good. Next time I hope we can forego the sweet and sour chicken. The long-term expense somehow loses its sweetness. In the meantime, let's see if we can trim the fat off our food spending and have something to invest before our financial cupboard becomes bare.

Example: A $9.25 Chinese take-out meal, invested over 20 years at 10% nets a growth of $7024.16. Keep that in mind the next time you order.

FOOD SAVINGS

PENNY PINCHER

$ _____ Use two 50-cent coupons.

$ _____ No cheese on a sandwich.

$ _____ No gourmet coffee!

$ _____ Save leftovers from the restaurant for next day.

$ _____ Eat a balanced breakfast to decrease snacking.

$ _____ Buy a store brand item.

$ _____ Buy one less name brand item.

$ _____ Pop old fashion popcorn kernels rather than microwave brands.

$ _____ Eat less meat on sandwiches.

$ _____ Eat less meat at dinner.

$ _____ Eat less meat at breakfast.

$ _____ Eat out during the "lunch" time menus.

$ _____ Omelet – use 2 jumbo eggs vs. 4 large ones.

$ _____ Skip a dinner per month.

$ _____ Skip a lunch per month.

$ _____ Save napkins at the restaurant (only the ones you initially take or are given.)

$ _____ Save napkins received at the drive-thru.

$ _____ Skip the chewing gum and mints.

$ _____ Skip a breakfast.

$ _____ Don't use recipes with strange ingredients you'll only use once.

$ _____ Take exact cash into the grocery store.

$ _____ Eat a bowl of cereal for dinner.

$ _____ Buy a smaller size of produce. (Read the label; a few less ounces can save precious pennies.)

$ _____ Buy a smaller size of meat. (Read the label; a few less ounces on this purchase can add a lot of meat to your finances!)

$ _____ Give up one favorite food for a month. (I put the coffeemaker in the laundry room one January just to see if I would miss my daily cup of coffee. The coffeemaker stayed there for over two years!)

$ _____ Use a dropper to add salad dressing to your salad.

$ _____ Buy off brand coffee.

$ _____ Buy a smaller size coffee/tea.

$ _____ Eat out only with a coupon.

$ _____ Join a food co-op.

$ _____ Keep resealable plastic bags with you. When you get a dessert or bagel, save it for a later meal.

$ _____ Buy medium eggs vs. large.

$ _____ Buy tofu instead of meat, and season it to your liking.

$ _____ Skip meat for a day.

$ _____ Buy fruit in season.

$ _____ Buy veggies in season.

$ _____ Buy smaller size ice cream or any type of dessert.

$ _____ Buy unshelled nuts.

$ _____ Buy unshelled shrimp.

$ _____ Save lemon peel in freezer for grated lemon peel.

$ _____ Save orange peel in freezer for grated orange peel.

$ _____ Make cookie dough in batches & freeze for future desserts.

$ _____ Avoid buying flavored water.

$ _____ Buy bagels/muffins in bunches and freeze.

$ _____ Shop on double/triple coupon day.

$ _____ If a soda fanatic, buy in bulk and take to work to avoid excess spending at the vending machine.

$ _____ Stick to your grocery list.

$ _____ Put one grocery item back before you check out at the register!

$ _____ Grow your own herbs.

$ _____ If you drink alcohol, consume one less drink.

$ _____ If you drink alcohol, purchase a less expensive brand.

$ _____ If you drink alcohol, give it up for a week. (You could also save a fortune if you quit altogether!)

$ _____ Skip extra dessert toppings.

$ _____ Skip extra toppings on sandwiches.

$ _____ Skip bread for one week.

$ _____ Add water to salad dressing bottles.

$ _____ Eat an apple for dinner.

$ _____ Eat leftover food from your freezer for a week.

$ _____ Use less milk on cereal.

$ _____ Skip the sweet beverage.

$ _____ Split the cost of dessert with a friend, spouse, or child.

$ _____ Decide on fast food order BEFORE placing it; don't respond to "will that be all?" and order more stuff.

$ _____ Skip one extra pizza topping.

$ _____ Order a pizza one size smaller than usual.

$ _____ Put a tad less sweetener in each serving.

$ _____ Take fresh popcorn for a snack.

$ _____ Add olive oil to salad dressing to stretch it.

$ _____ Skip the cute $2.00 mini desserts offered at restaurants.

$ _____ Add a little water to your milk.

$ _____ Eat a dinner mint vs. dessert.

$ _____ Use restaurant take out versus eating at the restaurant to avoid paying a tip. (Sorry, servers. If I'm dead broke, I won't be able to frequent your establishment in the future!)

$ _____ Don't use coupons that require purchase of a drink or dessert.

$ _____ Visit warehouse stores around lunch/dinner time for food samples.

$ _____ Hosting a large dinner party? Go to an all-inclusive buffet-style restaurant. There'll be no alcohol costs and desserts will be included.

$ _____ Your Idea - _____.

$ _____ Your Idea - _____.

$ _____ Your Idea - _____.

$ _____ TOTAL ANNUAL SAVINGS

· ELEVEN ·

Utilities: *Heat Down, Savings Up*

Turn off those lights. Quit running that water. Put on a sweater. Take off that sweater. Throw another blanket on the bed. These were phrases often uttered by my parents when I was growing up. In Virginia, we experienced all four seasons, so adjusting the thermostat to accommodate a family of six was a never-ending challenge.

Having lived through the Great Depression, my parents knew firsthand the agony of survival without the basic necessities of life. We were often reminded of those times when we were found wasting the precious natural resources allotted us. During my teen years, I grew up in an all-electric house. Each month when the electric bill arrived, time stood still while Dad grabbed for the nearest knife and slid it under the envelope flap. The contents either produced a sigh of relief or another month of lectures on the hard times when electricity didn't exist.

Dad was always overly concerned that the water level in our well might drop too low. I can now see the subtle frugal impact that it has had on my life, especially when I catch myself turning off the lights in public bathrooms!

Today, conservationists tell us to dim our lights, buy energy-efficient appliances, insulate our water heaters, and weather-strip our doors and windows. Chances are, we have already done most or all of these things. But it's the daily minute choices that slip through the cracks and can wreak havoc on utility costs, not to mention long-range retirement funds. We may not be able to influence the vote at the legislative house when the local public utility regulatory board seeks to justify rate hikes, but we can influence and regulate our *own* house. So, dim the lights, turn off the wide-screen, and find your utility leaks before the financial well runs dry.

> A one-degree drop on your thermostat can hardly be felt... except in your wallet!

UTILITIES SAVINGS

$ _____ Weather-strip around doors and windows.

$ _____ Turn up you're A/C setting by 1 degree. Turning it up more will increase savings even more!

$ _____ Turn down the hot water heater temperature when traveling.

$ _____ Turn down the heat setting by 1 degree.

$ _____ Keep vents free from being blocked to maintain proper airflow.

$ _____ Check ducts for leakage.

$ _____ Only run the dishwasher with full loads.

$ _____ Use cooler water for wash loads.

$ _____ Lower your hot water heater temperature; 120 degrees is adequate.

$ _____ Buy firewood off season.

$ _____ Have a candlelight dinner.

$ _____ Set a timer to raise heat in the house 30 minutes after you arrive home.

$ _____ Turn off more than one TV.

$ _____ Combine two small/medium size wash loads and dry one big one!

$ _____ Wash a load each week with cold water only.

$ _____ Rinse wash loads with cold water.

$ _____ Turn off the light if leaving the room more than five minutes.

$ _____ Turn off the heat at night and get out your grandma's quilt.

$ _____ Use a shorter washing machine *wash* time.

$ _____ Use less hot dryer setting time.

$ _____ Use a *cooler* dryer setting to dry. (Example – tumble dry vs. normal).

$ _____ Drop long distance on your home phone.

$ _____ Put a dimmer on bright lights (like in the dining room or den).

$ _____ Use a carpet sweeper instead of a vacuum.

$ _____ Chill in the air? Avoid turning on heat; put a heating pad on your neck/back to warm you up.

$ _____ Unplug your hair dryer, curling iron, and all other grooming appliances when not in use.

$ _____ In the summer, keep blinds closed to block sunlight entering the house.

$ _____ Don't buy oversized towels; they use too much water and electricity.

$ _____ Install a programmable thermostat.

$ _____ Unplug the TV when away from home.

$ _____ Unplug computers when away from home.

$ _____ Change your HVAC system's air filters to keep them running efficiently.

$ _____ Use the microwave to reduce stove or oven use.

$ _____ Use lower wattage light bulbs in one room.

$ _____ Set a timer to heat the house 15 minutes later in the morning.

$ _____ Turn off outside lights ASAP after waking up.

$ _____ Turn on outside lights 15 minutes later than usual at night.

$ _____ Never use artificial light when the sun will do.

$ _____ Run your ceiling fan at lower speed.

$ _____ Don't keep an auto-off iron plugged in.

$ _____ Your Idea - _____.

$ _____ Your Idea - _____.

$ _____ Your Idea - _____.

$ _____ TOTAL MONTHLY SAVINGS

· TWELVE ·

Gardening and Landscaping: *Dirt Ain't Dirt Cheap*

My childhood outdoors space came ready-made. As a youngster, the enormous acreage purchased by my Dad was underappreciated by me. Only as an adult have I realized the wealth that it bestowed. Our home was surrounded by sprawling trees, with a quaint little pond just a stone's throw from the sloped front yard. Our long, winding dirt driveway was lined with, what I thought was, a bunch of old trees.

As I grew older, I was enamored by all of the savory surroundings. The entrance to our driveway held a cluster of pear trees. As we traveled along, crossed the rickety bridge, and ascended the bend in the road, we were met with apple trees to the left. Several hundred feet ahead was our house, with a driveway turnaround and an old well pump planted in the center. Once we opened our chain-link fence and proceeded down the walkway, we were met by a huge hickory nut tree to the right. A cluster of peach trees were nestled along the fence's border on the right, and were just the right height for a tomboy to climb. Across the yard to the left was a rambling grapevine. (Don't tell anyone, but one year my uncle made a batch of wine.)

On the front of our house stood a lonely cherry tree. We managed to collect a few bowls of delicious fruit from it before my older brother decided to scale the puny branches, resulting in a modern-day George Washington fiasco, minus the hatchet. I can't recall the exact location of all of the remaining tasty treats, but I do remember each summer my family finding patches of wild blackberries and strawberries sprinkled throughout the property. Needless to say, we always looked forward to summer time!

Mom chose to stay at home until my youngest brother turned five and started kindergarten, so she had time to try her hand at developing a green thumb. We had the usual array of shrubbery throughout the property; after all, my Dad's college major was agronomy (the science of soil management and crop production). She also tried her hand at rose bushes until the reoccurrence of black spots all but ruined her beautiful yellow blossoms. Yes, the outdoors was amazing, but the indoors also overflowed with plants of all sizes littered throughout the house. This affinity towards the greener things in life followed me to the South.

Miss Lily and Me

When I completed college and settled in Atlanta, one of the first things I purchased to help christen my new apartment was a plant. My collection increased and decreased, based upon the consistency of my watering and fertilizing habits. I'll never forget the huge peace lily gifted to me by my coworkers at my first job's going-away party. Not wanting to kill this plant like I did the others, I asked one of the ladies how often I should water it. Her instructions were quite simple: "just put it in the shower with you once a week." This advice fit quite well with my left-brain tendencies, so every Saturday morning Miss Lily and I enjoyed our bath time. Her leaves were green and shiny. She grew wide and tall, for a season. Then Miss Lily began to shrivel. I couldn't pinpoint the problem. My protocol hadn't changed. The times in the shower weren't as frequent, but she always got a hefty bucket of water each week. No one offered any different directives. No one said to cut back on watering. I eventually got a clue what was wrong the day that a group of friends helped me to vacate my apartment, and my friend Susan picked up my Peace Lily to transport it. I hadn't watered it in over a week in preparation for the move, yet Susan got drenched right in the pants. My beautiful Lily began to turn brown and drop her leaves. She couldn't be saved. I had over watered her. That was my first and last botanical bathroom debacle.

I don't do well with the cactus species either. I water them and they die. I let them dry out and they die. I fertilize them and they die. I think it's a personal vendetta against me. I can't say that I miss them. They don't grow fast enough for me; besides, I hate any type of splintery intrusion, especially the invisible kind.

Weeds, Water Woes, and War

When you own a home, you don't need indoor plants that flourish. You do, however, need grass and shrubbery. My first home was just what I prayed for: a split level with a stone veneer, 3 bedrooms, 2 baths, a small eat-in kitchen, a den with a fireplace, and a one-car garage. The house was only two years old, so it was virtually brand new. The builder had planted the usual shrubbery along the front elevation. A group of red tip bushes lined the right border, and an island of azalea bushes rested beneath the front-yard pine trees. Grass was there; I just had to cut it. I bought the home in October, so the dipping Autumn temperatures caused the grass to lie dormant until the Spring. I didn't have to gear up for lawn maintenance for several months.

When the signs of Spring began to emerge, I spotted thick green blades shooting up underneath another cluster of trees in the front yard. Within a few short weeks the most beautiful yellow blooms appeared. I had daffodils! The former owner must have planted them. My yard had lots of colors! Yellow daffodils. Pink and white azaleas. Red tips. Green grass. I soon discovered the meaning of perennials, so I welcomed their effortless return each year. The red tips grew and grew without any effort on my part (until a young couple's speeding car jumped the curb late one night, wiping out half of the bushes!) The azaleas seemed to have a mind of their own, although they needed an occasional pruning.

Then there's the lawn; the tall Fescue grass. Lawns are another story. They start out so green and plush. They desire to mimic the most scenic golf course. They have so much potential, but they have an archenemy called weeds. Remember how and where I grew up. Dad had many mouths to feed, so despite his agronomy degree, he wasn't about to waste money on a weed-free lawn. He knew what was important. Reap a harvest from the ground and make the rest a groundcover to keep the terrain from washing away. I never knew that grass needed to be fed with nitrogen, phosphorus, and potassium. Those were merely symbols from my 9th grade physical science class. So, back in Atlanta, weeds began to encroach upon my beautiful Fescue and the fight was on. I de-weeded. I fertilized. I aerated. I re-seeded. I watered. I even added lime. On and on it went. I cut the grass high. I cut the grass low. I let the grass grow thick. I sharpened the lawnmower blade so it wouldn't tear the grass blades. Oh, how I pampered that lawn.

I was able to keep many weeds at bay and the lawn fairly even and green, but one unexpected event changed that. Several years after I had moved in, something unusual kept reoccurring. Every day when I walked to the mailbox, I noticed that someone's car-washing water was running into my yard. (This was years before our county issued a ban on outdoor watering.) As the days went by, it finally dawned on me that other yards didn't have water pooling in front of them.

The Soggy Truth

One afternoon, while dodging the muddy accumulation near my mailbox, I had an unpleasant thought; one that caused me to replay a scene in my neighbor's yard. They had to dig up their front yard due to substandard PVC water pipes that had burst. I quickly called the water company, at which time they informed me that my current water usage was way over the top. Bingo! A pipe leak! A plumber was called, the entry point of the leakage was located, and a trench from the house to the street was dug. The repair was made without too much damage in my wallet, but dirt that's been dug up *never* goes back in the same way. And I suppose weeds are always waiting to surface when you flip the soil over. That's been almost two decades ago, and my perfectly even terrain has never been the same.

While I was making every effort to fight the front lawn demons, they were attacking from the back. Trees. More trees. Trees with leaves and pine straw. Leaves by *themselves* are easy to rake against the fence and allow to decompose overtime. Pine straw is even easy when you can rake and spread it beneath shrubs and around flower beds; but leaves and pine straw *together* do not mix. They are heavy to move and useless in landscaping. So, what's a single woman to do with piles of this mixture? Two choices: have it hauled away or rake it against the foundation and under the trees. Being a frugal female, I was not about to spend any money to haul off this never-ending shower of arboreal debris. I settled for raking it against the foundation and around the trees, being ever so careful to leave a gap near the tree trunks to avoid rot. (The peace lily fiasco stayed with me.) This technique worked well for several years, and I was even able to begin filling in a gaping hole that had begun to form in the backyard.

Only the Neighbor Knows

One sunny afternoon, I had an over-the-fence conversation with my neighbor, Brad. He and his wife Courtney had moved to the neighborhood when it was primarily wooded. He recounted the order in which homes sprang up. He even pointed out the entire litany of neighborhood flaws, including the off-centered road paving that crested at the top of the hill, and the backwards installation of all dining room sliding doors. (I always wondered why the screen was on the *inside* of the door!) He then pointed down the alley of every backyard and revealed the cause of the subtle change in everyone's landscape; the builder had buried construction debris, and it had rotted over time. That was the reason for my backyard gaping hole!

It Grows and Goes

Somewhere in the middle of my working career years, I had a three-year stint when I was in and out of Atlanta, and my home (and the lawn) were left in the hands of renters. Upon my return, I recall the husband speaking of his determination to "get the yard in shape." He seeded and reseeded. The lawn was so thick that the neighbors were congratulating him on its lushness. I believe he transformed it into something spectacular beautiful. After all, I had experienced it firsthand years before. But no matter how lush a lawn looks, weeds love the ground and seek to make their appearance on every turn. On top of that, no matter how much nitrogen, phosphorus, and potassium you have in your arsenal, it won't make a hill of beans difference if a delivery truck with mag wheels stays parked on the lawn each day. (That's another book for another day.)

Do I need to go on and on with the drudgery of landscaping battles? I applaud anyone who has a green thumb and knows what they're doing. Hats off to those who can plant, prune, re-seed, and actually see the fruit of their labor. (Oh, I forgot to mention my initial bulb-planting effort. I planted them upside down!)

> Please don't exhaust your wallet while striving to maintain a magazine-manicured lawn.

Can we all agree that gardening and landscaping can be extremely costly? The outdoors cannot be left to itself. (Even perennials need to be divided from time to time, provided they're planted in the right direction.) Thorns and thistles have been with Man since the Garden of Eden and will continue to plague and force us to *work by the sweat of our brows*. So please don't exhaust your wallet while striving to maintain a magazine-manicured lawn. You will never get your snowball rolling if you resort to running to the local nursery and loading your little red wagon with everything on the shelf. Do all the research you can on simplifying this process. I'm in the trenches with you. Our lawns should be kept presentable. We certainly can't wait until time to sell our homes to try to de-weed or resurface.

That's when we make costly mistakes and start considering budget-killing options like sod. The less grass for a groundcover, the better. The less trees to tend to, the better. The more repeat business (a.k.a. perennials), the better. There are ways to spend less outdoors, so there will be more *inside* our wallets. We just have to keep digging up ways to weed out unnecessary items. Pretty soon you'll see your financial snowball picking up speed, and you'll have your retirement savings made in the shade.

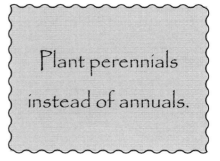

Plant perennials instead of annuals.

GARDENING and LANDSCAPING SAVINGS

$ _____ Plant trees/shrubs to shade your house.

$ _____ Use newspaper around flowers to reduce weeds; cover with mulch.

$ _____ Rake up pine-straw in your yard or your neighbor's and use as mulch.

$ _____ Do your own lawnmower maintenance.

$ _____ Leave your landscaping to the birds and bees, as many plants/flowers have sprung up in my yard due to pollination!

$ _____ Toss out grass seeds each time you mow the lawn to reduce bare spots and avoid erosion.

$ _____ Plant flowers, grass seeds, and shrubbery when rain is in the extended forecast.

$ _____ Water outdoor flowers/plants with inside shower water.

$ _____ Choose drought-resistant plants.

$ _____ Plant perennials instead of annuals.

$ _____ Buy smaller indoor and outdoor plants.

$ _____ Cover weeds with plastic to kill them.

$ _____ Buy lawn stuff at the end of the season.

$ _____ Buy outdoor furniture at the end of the season. (That's when I bought the infamous grill, the one in the living room!)

$ _____ Prune your own low-hanging tree limbs! I did mine with the help of my friend Cindy, a ladder, and extended handle pruning shears. (I hope the neighbors weren't watching!)

$ _____ Check with local schools for horticulture class plant sales.

$ _____ Buy bedding plants/shrubs towards the end of the season.

$ _____ Plan do-it-yourself aeration with a neighbor and split the cost of renting the machine.

$ _____ Schedule house pressure washing service with a neighbor and split the machine rental cost.

$ _____ Cut your neighbor's grass for a buck! Perhaps they'll return the favor one day.

$ _____ Choose annuals that tend to reseed.

$ _____ Ask a neighbor for a clipping of a plant for your yard or house.

$ _____ Get off that riding mower and use a push mower. Sell it!!!

$ _____ Make your own lawn edger; you can use an array of materials, such as slats from old venetian blinds that bend.

$ _____ Your Idea - _____.

$ _____ Your Idea - _____.

$ _____ Your Idea - _____.

$ _____ TOTAL ANNUAL SAVINGS

Start a social chat group to discover the least costly methods for maintaining a lawn and growing your own food.

· THIRTEEN ·

Car Savings: *Rev It Up*

The words flew out of my mouth before I knew it. I hadn't planned to say them, but in retrospect, they had been lying dormant in my subconscious for years.

During the 80's and 90's, my job included hours of drive time between schools, not including the drive home after work. One of my favorite radio shows during my drive home was hosted by nationally known consumer advocate, Clark Howard. Each day I anticipated hearing new tidbits of information to help me withstand the constant but subtle onslaught of financial bandits. Sometimes his comments were quite amusing, like the time he bragged about his $3.00 designer suit find. But most of his airtime was devoted to helping the little man (and woman).

One day, Clark got on the topic of buying a car, and the added fees that dealerships cleverly pass on to the unsuspecting customer. He made mention of the alleged "administrative fee" that is tacked on to the cost of cars, whether new or used. His statement didn't catch my attention. His *analogy* did. He likened it to a department store levying an extra charge on every purchase to offset their utility bills. My immediate response was, "that's ridiculous!" I'm sure you just responded the same way. At that time in my life, I was not in the market for a vehicle. In fact, I was still on my second car. And if the life of that one was anything like the first, I could count on another 100,000 miles before the wheels would fall off. (By the way, that second car carried me over 202,000 miles and was still going strong when I donated it.) So, that afternoon, I just stored Clark's little car-buyer *beware* tip deep within my gray matter and went on with life.

Then it happened in 1999. I accepted a therapist assignment in New Mexico. The thought of making a 1400-mile cross-country trip in a car with high mileage and the engine light on was out of the question. I began the arduous task of identifying the most reliable vehicles at the most affordable prices. (After all, this is what the consumer advocate had taught me!) Unbeknownst to me, some of the luxury car brands had undergone major body style redesigns, and loyal car-owners were dumping the old styles for the new. Hence, the used models were now in my price range. After some extensive homework, I narrowed my selections to two makes located at three dealerships close in proximity to one another.

I spent a few days running back and forth between dealerships, located within a few miles of each other. All vehicles drove quite well, with more bells and whistles than I ever thought existed or would ever use. Fortunately, none of the salesmen were pushy. I guess they were taken aback by this single woman who was not impressed with the tire rims or leather interior, but was more concerned with the leg room in the backseat and the size of the trunk. Remember, I was embarking upon a long road trip, and I needed to be my own mover. (It pays to do one's homework, because 20 years later, both makes and models proved to be extremely reliable.)

After a week or two of revisiting all three dealerships, I decided to purchase a Volvo®. Of the two I had driven, I chose the one with less miles. The sales guy at dealership number one insisted that I keep my "alleged" new green Volvo® for a day, so I happily spun off behind the wheel; only, I found myself driving down the road to dealership number two, where the black Volvo® was located. The mileage was higher in that car, but the price was $1000 less. After one last test drive, I made the decision to purchase the black one, and the salesman agreed to drive the green car back to his competitor.

Test-Driven

Now it was time to close the deal. I had already researched prices, so I was not about to engage in the good cop/bad cop theatrics of salesmen running back and forth to sales managers. (I fell for that during my first car purchase.) Haggling over a trade-in amount or getting trapped in the dealership's inflated financing would not be factors in this equation. I already had my down payment and pre-approved financing from my credit union, along with a ballpark figure of my monthly notes. We just needed to get on with the formalities.

After the test drive, we entered the showroom and the salesman kindly beckoned me to have a seat in a nearby chair. He offered me a soft drink while he arranged the necessary paperwork on the table. While I sipped on my drink, he wrote in the figures and gently rotated the papers towards me for my review. I leaned forward and began to follow his finger meticulously as he moved down the carbon-copy document, outlining the rationale for each numerical entry.

The cost of the car was not disputed. The hefty down-payment was subtracted. As much as we'd all like to, we cannot escape tag and registration fees, nor that dreaded state tax (unless you live in a tax-free state), so those numbers were not disputed. I was rolling right along with my mild-mannered, soft-spoken salesman, nearing the end of the form, when he said, "this is the administrative fee…" It was **$300!** Ding, ding, ding! Bells and whistles went off! Beware! Beware! This does not compute! Like a freshly rehearsed line from a movie, my knee-jerk response was, "I don't want to pay it." The

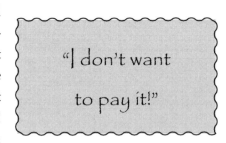

"I don't want to pay it!"

salesman was briefly stunned, but calmly stated that it was a fee included in all purchases. I reiterated, "I don't want to pay it." He restated the dealership's policy that all cars must have this fee included. I restated, "I don't want to pay it."

Now, I must stop and let you in on an undisclosed fact. I was **extremely** shy throughout childhood and into adulthood. Growing up as the only girl in a family of four kids, I played by myself quite often. I remember one day in kindergarten sitting in a corner reading books while the other girls played in the kitchen area. Grade school and high school years were a little more liberating, but I still held the reputation for being shy. Even college did not move me to become a jabber-jaw; and I *never* volunteered to speak out in class. So, when Little Miss Shy Girl stood her ground that day, it was completely out of character.

> Is your spending so out of control that you can't accelerate your savings?

I suppose the comforting factor was that I was in the driver's seat. (No pun intended.) I had a down payment. I had pre-approved financing. I had researched prices. I was not desperate for a car, least of all *that* car. Remember, I had driven to that Volvo® dealership (number two) from dealership number one, in dealership *one's* car! The salesman knew that I could just as easily have jumped back into that car and driven back to number one's store to make the purchase. So, after a few moments of silence, the salesman offered to reduce the purchase price by $300, to which I agreed.

Sometimes I have a habit of replaying events in my head. Why didn't I at least counter the sticker price? After all, another $300 off would have been a nice round number, wouldn't you agree? Well, you can't win them all; but I won *that* one, on *that* hot August day. In fact, I think everyone ought to have at least one-upmanship story in their life.

Enough of my story. What's driving up *your* car costs? Is your spending so out of control that you can't accelerate your savings? Like gas fumes from a nozzle, what dollars are escaping from *your* wallet? Perhaps my list will help you put the brakes on over spending and help kick your savings into high gear.

 **Example:** If you were to purchase a $15,000 car versus a $30,000 one, the difference invested for 20 years at 10% growth equals $109,000. How much is a smooth ride worth?

REVVED UP CAR SAVINGS
(This also applies to trucks, SUVs and all moving objects with wheels!)

$ _____ Walk somewhere instead of driving.

$ _____ Car pool to work.

$ _____ Car pool to the movies or any entertainment event.

$ _____ Sell your new car and buy a reliable used car instead.

$ _____ Use a coupon for an oil change.

$ _____ Use an app to locate the best priced gasoline.

$ _____ Bundle car repairs to decrease labor costs. (I sustained some hideous scratches on the top of my first Subaru. A while later, I was hit from behind and had extensive damage. When I went to get an estimate at the body shop, I asked the owner what he would charge to paint the top. His estimate was close to $200. The last words he said to me before I left was, "If you bring your car back here to have the work done, I'll paint the top for free." (Guess which body shop got my business?)

$ _____ Air fresheners – put perfumed oil drops in a tiny dish and leave in the car.

$ _____ Extend your oil change 250 miles past the recommended time.

$ _____ Ladies, go on "special oil change day."

$ _____ Park and go inside the bank vs. idling in the drive-thru.

$ _____ Park and go inside the restaurant vs. idling in the drive-thru.

$ _____ Keep car oil at the proper level.

$ _____ Keep transmission fluid at the proper level.

$ _____ Keep coolant tapped out.

$ _____ Ride to work one cool day without using heat.

$ _____ Ride to work one warm day without using A/C.

$ _____ Pay for gas with cash to "feel" the amount spent. (Some gas stations even charge you a fee for using debit or credit cards.)

$ _____ When given the option, skip valet parking and park it yourself!

$ _____ Downsize your car.

$_____ No tailgating and sudden braking. It can wear out brake pads faster.

$_____ Don't pay to have your car bulbs put in if you have the tools and ability to access them.

$_____ Install your own windshield wipers.

$_____ Don't get a custom license plate.

$_____ Skip one car errand.

$_____ Opt out of "new car" fragrance with a car wash unless it's free.

$_____ Don't speed; you get better gas mileage that way.

$_____ Vacuum your car at home vs. paying for it.

$_____ Shop car insurance annually. Let your agent know that you're doing it. (I did this once and got an instant reduction in premium.)

$_____ Keep the trunk free of unnecessary cargo that could cause the car to use more gas.

$_____ Buy blind spot mirrors; they may help you avoid an accident.

$_____ Ladies, check your makeup before leaving home or the office; save that makeup mirror light bulb.

$_____ If you're almost due for the regular car maintenance, don't have a separate oil change done. That's usually part of the maintenance cost.

$_____ Make your next car purchase one with smaller tires.

$_____ Research average maintenance costs before buying your next car.

$_____ Wax your own car.

$_____ Keep battery cables clean to extend battery life.

$_____ Change your own car's air filter, if you can reach it.

$_____ Select a cheaper car wash package deal.

$_____ Get a second opinion on car repairs and let both locations know that you're doing this.

$_____ Use a mechanic other than the dealer for a better rate on labor.

$_____ Pay car insurance in full to avoid monthly partial payment fees.

$_____ You have no car fresheners? Open windows and let fresh air in.

$_____ Get home before dark to save car light bulbs.

$ _____ Don't pay "administrative" fees when buying a car.

$ _____ Paying cash for gas? Take the exact change inside the gas station to avoid buying snacks.

$ _____ Increase your collision deductible to the highest deductible (once you have the deductible amount saved.)

$ _____ Increase your comprehensive deductible (once you have the deductible amount saved.)

$ _____ Skip one car wash per year.

$ _____ Use school or church fund-raising car washes.

$ _____ Use cruise control on long trips.

$ _____ Don't buy premium gas unless recommended by the manufacturer.

$ _____ Learn to parallel park and not hit the curb (wearing out tires faster!)

$ _____ Buy tires at locations that offer free lifetime rotation.

$ _____ Don't circle a parking lot looking for the closest space; park the car!

$ _____ In the summer, run errands before it gets too hot, avoiding the use of A/C.

$ _____ Don't use your car's A/C the first hot week of the season.

$ _____ Find shortcuts to destinations.

$ _____ Take routes with less red lights where idling can occur.

$ _____ NEVER trade in your car; sell it yourself.

$ _____ When at the gas station, discard your car's trash to reduce the amount of trash and need for trash bags at home.

$ _____ Paying car insurance in monthly installments? Double up one month to save the monthly charge.

$ _____ Coast towards red lights. They may turn green and you won't have to brake or idle.

$ _____ Fill up the tank EVERY time gas prices dip; they may be back up when you would normally fill up.

$ _____ Take routes with less traffic.

$ _____ Leave for work earlier to avoid sitting in traffic.

$ _____ Leave a venue earlier or after the crowds have left to avoid idling and wasting gas.

$ _____ Your Idea_____.

$ _____ Your Idea_____.

$ _____ Your Idea_____.

$ _____ TOTAL ANNUAL SAVINGS

FOURTEEN

Entertainment, Hobbies, and Holidays:
Fun is not Funny

The cost of American entertainment has risen to new heights. In fact, Paul Bond, in his 2013 article on the Global Entertainment Industry, predicted that by 2017, Americans would fund almost 30% of this entire Industry, *worldwide*![21]

Let's glance at another industry; the savings industry. An article by The Motley Fool's Sean Williams reported in 2016 that nearly 70% of all Americans had less than $1000 in savings.[22] Fast forward to 2018 and the numbers have not improved significantly. In fact, 58% of those surveyed admitted that they have less than $1,000 in the bank. Did you just assume the dog head-tilt posture? The figures are out of kilter, aren't they? I can remember when movie admissions cost 50 cents. Today, you can't buy a 3-ounce box of candy for that amount. I also remember going to the premiere of a Vietnam-themed movie in 1981 with my brother, only to discover that the admission fee was $5.00. I must have blacked out over the price, because I don't recall ever having bought any refreshments. Fast forward to 2016 when Anthony and I cleared our calendars to catch a movie at the local "dollar" theater (which had raised its admission to $3.) Our total bill was $17, and we shared a bucket of popcorn and drank tap water! Forget the theater; pretty soon it'll be cheaper to fly to Hollywood and catch a live filming.

The Painful Splurge

On our last Christmas get-away we decided that we would splurge. Throughout the year, we had managed to save a sizeable amount in our food budget, giving us a whopping surplus to spend at the beach. Our motto for the week would be, "have fun." That's normal, right? Doesn't America love to have fun? Then why was I shocked over the senior citizen price of the latest Sci-Fi premiere? And from what reservoir did the theater siphon its bottled liquid to warrant a four-dollar price tag? You've never seen a 60-year-old woman clutch her popcorn bucket so tightly, as if it were the latest designer purse. I vowed not to drop this hefty aromatic representation of a $34 afternoon of fun. My husband got his wish to see the premiere. I got my buttered popcorn, my gold-laden water, and two naps. (I'm *not* a Sci-Fi fan. And by the way, when *will* the last return *really* be the last?)

Next day's fun-in-the-sun time landed us inside. The South experienced freezing temperatures that week, prompting us to hang out at the local bowling alley instead of weathering the elements in inadequate attire. Given the previous day's sticker shock at the movie house, why did my knees buckle and eyes roll when the man behind the counter offered us an hour of bowling in a private room, the *only* available space, for a whopping $24.50? Even worse, we conceded to take it! We managed to hit a strike or two, but guess what couple bowled three straight games without sipping an ounce of water or taking one bite of a frankfurter! With prices like these, it's hard to have fun!

As a child, my family's most memorable (and probably most costly) trip was to the 1964 New York World's Fair®. I don't recall my parents hovering over the kitchen table, conjuring up a plan to fund our family extravaganza. After all, we were a middle-class family with one breadwinner (on a teacher's salary, I might add.) I don't remember them fretting over the credit card bill later. They must have counted the cost before we hit the road, so there was no bill upon our return. What made it so affordable? Perhaps it was the car ride versus plane tickets, or eating Mommy's fried chicken in the hotel room versus dining at a restaurant. Then again, in the sixties, the racially discriminant climate, no doubt, limited my parents' options. Nevertheless, the expense of our trip never followed us home.

Let's face it. We all want to enjoy ourselves, whether we're on a Saturday afternoon outing, a weekend resort, or a Mediterranean cruise. We all desire healthy outlets to unwind from the stressors of life. Making small choices can keep lots of dollars in our pockets without placing a damper on the fun.

And while we're on the subject of fun, let's visit an issue that could make or break us. Amusement parks, carnivals, and fairs can be a great deal of fun. (There's that word again.) They have entertainment for every member of the family, from dare-devil rollercoaster rides to blueberry pie contests. There is so much to enjoy. But did you realize that one thing is usually lacking at these venues? Our brains! Did you know that the definition of *muse* is "to become absorbed in thought".[23] So, if we are being *amused*, we are not thinking, we are just *doing*. And chances are, we're not giving much thought to our spending either!

> When we are amused we're not giving much thought to our spending.

Hobby expenses need to be put in check as well. In fact, some so-called businesses are just that. If it doesn't turn a profit it's a hobby. Accept it, enjoy it, but don't fool yourself into musing that you have a business. Make it profitable or call it what it is, and limit your spending to support it.

Black Friday Frenzy & Beyond

The holiday season in November and December can be another "amusing" time when gray matter comes totally unglued. Is it any wonder that the merchants are biting their nails to see whether Black Friday is a bang or bust? While they seek to cross the finish line in the *black*, most families go deeper into debt, not counting the cost. The only ones left smiling are the merchants. We buy stuff "just because," only to ask ourselves when the bills arrive, "*what was I thinking*?" You weren't! Slow down and think before you act.

Don't get caught up in the buying frenzy. If the store runs out of Junior's favorite computer game, believe me he'll survive. If he doesn't, well, it would have been a wasted purchase *anyway*. (Just kidding.)

Let's take a moment and walk through this holiday buying-craze. Put your credit card down and let's have a heart-to-heart talk. The giant retailers in America hang their success or failure on one day out of the year. Imagine having to wait 364 days to determine whether the CEO gets paid. (Actually, the CEO *always* manages to cut a check; it's the hard-working store employees who are sweating it out; people just like you and me.) And have you noticed lately the barrage of offers at the checkout counter? Offers like 20% off your entire purchase with a store credit card, cash bucks on future purchases, or a whopping 2% cash rewards program? Can I give you a quick math lesson? I know I'm way off track, but so might your spending be. What is 2% of $1000? The answer is $20, the equivalent of one Andrew Jackson bill. So, in order to partake of this special offer and slip Andy back into your alligator wallet, you would have to relinquish ten Ben Franklins. Ten! Let that resonate in the crevices of your mind. I give away one-thousand dollars…one-thousand dollars…**one thousand dollars**…and I get **$20** back. Are you kidding me? If you told a group of kids on Halloween that you would give each of them 5 pieces of candy back if they handed over their entire sugary loot, what do you think they would say? Probably, "no way!" So why are we acting worse than children?

In a June 1928 column by syndicated humorist Robert Quillen, he labelled the expression, "Americanism," as "using money you haven't earned to buy things you don't need to impress people you don't like."[24] This sounds almost identical to an earlier quote, doesn't it? I would venture to guess that folks in the early 1900's also had a problem with consumerism. In the 21st century, we have multiplied its devastating effects exponentially. People from a variety of industries have used this quote in an attempt to awaken us to the real ploy: advertising. It has its vast variations. Advertising is not simply glancing at an electronic billboard or viewing a million-dollar 30-second commercial during a major sports broadcast. Advertising is the gentle art of persuading the public to believe they want something that they don't need. It's not intrusive; it's gentle, and persuasive, *highly* persuasive. How persuasive? So much so that my almost non-verbal special-needs Pre-K student can ride past the golden arches and yell, "French-fries!"

> Advertising is the gentle art of persuading the public to believe they want something that they don't need.

Before I leave you at the cash register with that overflowing buggy of Belgian chocolates, silk scarves, and electronic devices, can we agree on one thing? Most gifts are over-rated and under-appreciated. You don't agree? Then put this book down, text your top five gift recipients, and ask them to name all the gifts that you gave them last Christmas. Maybe one of them will recall one or two items on the list. The rest are probably forgotten. Is this beginning to help you put things into perspective? I hope so, for your budget's sake. For your retirement years' sake. Even for your *children's* retirement years' sake.

Remember the earlier statistics that predicted Americans would shoulder one-third of the entire world's entertainment industry's costs? That figure may not be that unsettling until you realize that we are only 23%, of the world's total estimated 7.5 billion population.[25] I can only surmise that the 2018 stats will be even higher!

While our per capita expenses for fun and games supersede those of the entire world, so do our health care and nursing home costs! Contrary to belief by many Americans, there are **limits** to Medicare-funded services.[26] I speak from experience. You read earlier just a snippet of my Dad's needs during his 17-month health decline. And just in case you're banking on a Medicaid windfall to cover your and your loved ones' care, qualification for these services are based solely on strict asset and income limits. This quote should shed some gut-wrenching light: "A rule of thumb for the year 2018 is a single individual's income must be less than $2,250/month, and their resources, excluding their home and vehicle, must be valued at less than $2,000."[27] Coverage can vary from state to state, so do your research long before you think you or your loved ones may need this service.[28] Any concerns that you have may be best answered by an elder care attorney. (No, that's not a leader at your church, it's a lawyer!) I can only assume that with our steadily aging population, qualifications in the future will only become stricter than a tightly-wound rubber band.

Now, before you write me off as the greatest American entertainment killjoy, hear me out. Most forms of entertainment and holidays involve people, lots of people. But they don't have to break the bank to be enjoyable. My millennial and Generation X readers may not be able to relate, but at least you baby boomers can remember engaging in good, clean fun without uniforms, umpires, and organized teams. A party of two can have a great deal of cost-free fun. From time to time, even a quiet night of solitaire works for a single person.

Once upon a time, we were a creative bunch. Even babies would instinctively grab a pot and wooden spoon and have a bang-up time. When moms used to tell us to go outside and play (without getting into too much mischief), we'd set up obstacle courses, scale fences, climb trees, and ride bikes. When we got tired, we turned to nature and made an assortment of mud pies with rocks, twigs, and other earthy substances within our reach. (Who's willing to admit that they tasted one or two?) On a summer's evening when the sun began to set, we caught lightning bugs, crowded them into a mason jar, and punched holes in the lid for air holes, while we proudly held our nature-made flashlight. (I apologize to my city slickers. You haven't a clue what I'm talking about!)

Whether you grew up in the city, suburbs, or country, you have the capacity to entertain yourself without the aid of a handheld device. It won't kill you to give your thumbs a rest from gaming for one evening, not to mention those neck muscles that are being overly stretched from looking down too long! (Oops; the therapist in me is showing.) So, let's get back into the driver seat of our spending and steer those precious dollars back into our wallets, rather than watch them fly over the side of a roller coaster. You'll have ups and downs, but when the ride is over, from a financial standpoint, you'll have something to show for it.

Stay home and read a book.

ENTERTAINMENT and HOLIDAY SAVINGS

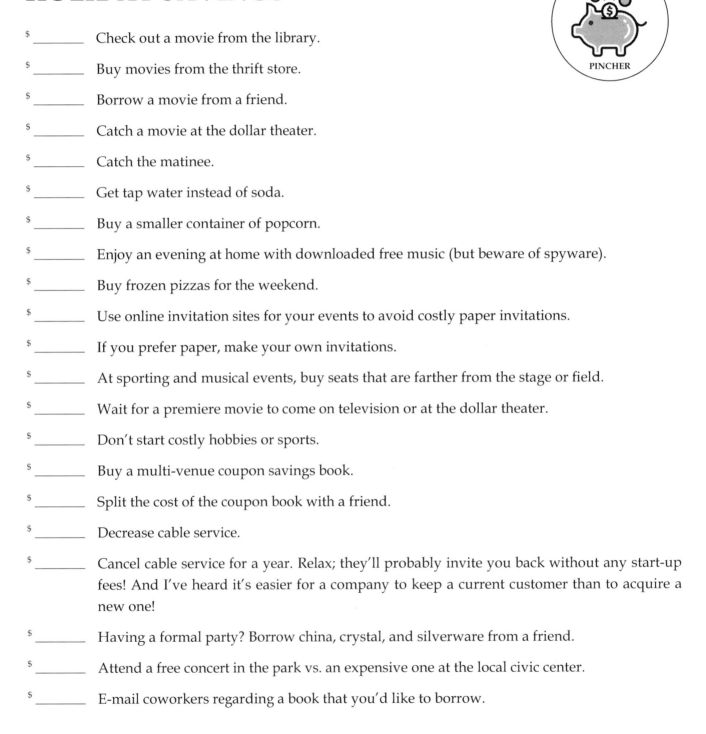

$ _____   Check out a movie from the library.

$ _____   Buy movies from the thrift store.

$ _____   Borrow a movie from a friend.

$ _____   Catch a movie at the dollar theater.

$ _____   Catch the matinee.

$ _____   Get tap water instead of soda.

$ _____   Buy a smaller container of popcorn.

$ _____   Enjoy an evening at home with downloaded free music (but beware of spyware).

$ _____   Buy frozen pizzas for the weekend.

$ _____   Use online invitation sites for your events to avoid costly paper invitations.

$ _____   If you prefer paper, make your own invitations.

$ _____   At sporting and musical events, buy seats that are farther from the stage or field.

$ _____   Wait for a premiere movie to come on television or at the dollar theater.

$ _____   Don't start costly hobbies or sports.

$ _____   Buy a multi-venue coupon savings book.

$ _____   Split the cost of the coupon book with a friend.

$ _____   Decrease cable service.

$ _____   Cancel cable service for a year. Relax; they'll probably invite you back without any start-up fees! And I've heard it's easier for a company to keep a current customer than to acquire a new one!

$ _____   Having a formal party? Borrow china, crystal, and silverware from a friend.

$ _____   Attend a free concert in the park vs. an expensive one at the local civic center.

$ _____   E-mail coworkers regarding a book that you'd like to borrow.

$_____ E-mail coworkers regarding a video that you'd like to borrow. (I know; they're quickly disappearing.)

$_____ Make your own Christmas decorations. (Make an extra one and sell it!)

$_____ Make corsages for school dances.

$_____ Celebrate your birthday at a restaurant that offers a free meal to the birthday patron.

$_____ In the market for a new TV? Buy a slightly smaller size than you really want.

$_____ Getting married? Make your own favors.

$_____ At the movies, split a combo meal with a friend.

$_____ Eat before going to the movies or sporting event. Every little savings helps.

$_____ Choose a sporting event with less expensive tickets or food or both!

$_____ Catch a bus or use an on-demand transportation service such as Uber® or Lyft® to get to a sporting or concert event.

$_____ Treat kids to an ice cream cone after a movie if they share popcorn & don't get candy. (Or figure out the best way to treat them while saving money at the theater.)

$_____ Avoid "voting" by text on TV contests where you will incur a phone charge.

$_____ Switch cable service when they have the next special offer.

$_____ Do hotdog night vs. pizza.

$_____ Your Idea! _____.

$_____ Your Idea! _____.

$_____ Your Idea! _____.

$_____ TOTAL ANNUAL SAVINGS

Cancel cable service for a year.

· FIFTEEN ·

Gifts and Shopping Galore: *A Rebate of Debt*

Have you ever read a book about the development of Americans' shopping habits? I haven't, but they must surely start in infancy! Consuming stuff is innate. After toddlers learn to say "mama" and "dada," one of their most important next words is "Gimme."

I don't recall how old I was. I couldn't have been much more than a toddler myself. With my right arm stretched high to reach my Momma's hand, I stumbled along beside her on Sycamore Street in downtown Petersburg, Virginia. The object of my desire can't be visualized. The details of my verbal request escape me. I only remember that I had wanted a doll, Mom had said *no*, and I walked along the sidewalk in my white leather lace-ups, with tears quietly streaming down my cheeks.

It's a given. We all love to shop. We do it online, at the mega-mall, the strip mall, and flea markets; even in church basement rummage sales. We shop because it makes us feel good. We shop because it's Friday. We shop because it's Wednesday. We shop because it's *any* day!

We have mastered the art of justifying every purchase: It's a 2-for-1 sale. It's Wednesday's markdown. I have a 20% off coupon. There's an additional savings with a store credit card. The list goes on and on. What's the most striking marketing phrase that nudges *you* towards the mall? Or for those who prefer to "save" by shopping online, what gets you dragging and clicking your way to debt? Is it the deceptive photography that makes a simple blouse from China look like a tailored original from Paris? Or is it the countdown timer in the bottom corner of the screen that urges you to make a quick buy before the special runs out?

> It's time to drop the "shop 'til you drop" mindset. The more we shop, the more our future savings drop out of sight.

Why do we keep making designer strangers rich? Beats me. Maybe we need something new and flashy to impress our friends. Or perhaps these overpriced threads raise our egos a few more notches. Come on, guys and girls, can we get a handle on this? When was the last time there was designer label comparison at the nursing home? The day shift worker who'll tend to your needs won't care what the label says. He or she will only be concerned that you have a clean shirt and pair of pants in the closet to put on you. And I hate to say it, but many niceties belonging to nursing home residents end up disappearing. It's time to drop the "shop 'til you drop" mindset. The more we shop, the more our future savings drop out of sight.

I've already addressed in an earlier chapter the overrating of gifts. It's a wonderful thing to give. We are even commanded in the Bible to do so. Many who don't even ascribe to its Truths have open hands and hearts to bless others. Americans are known as the most generous people in the world, especially when a horrific disaster strikes. So, let's distinguish between the two. Philanthropic giving is one thing. In this book, I'm talking about the gift-giving frenzy that has no plan, no purpose, and no end in sight. All we need is a wedding invitation, a funding request, or the news of a pregnancy or adoption, and off we go, grabbing the biggest buggy in the store. Christmas is the crescendo of all giving, yet its shockwaves linger throughout the year. Can we put the brakes on for a hot minute?!?

Let's talk value. Let's talk sentiment. Let's talk about the essence of gifting from the heart. I have a niece named Ariana. She just began her second year in college; Pre-Med. What a brain. Straight A's throughout her entire schooling career. Never missed a day of school, not even to attend her Senior Trip.

When Ariana was about five, she and her parents visited my church for a special evening program. When they drove up and she saw me, she leaped out of the car and in haste made her way towards me. As we embraced, she couldn't wait to tell me the news. Her little hand slid from behind her, holding the most exquisite metallic magenta-colored gift box. Its miniature size, with an even tinier yellow bow, made it even more special. She proudly announced that she had a gift for me. As my face lit up and I reached for this token of her love, Ariana's mom whispered a word of caution not to get my hopes up too high. When I lifted the lid, I uncovered the most beautiful black hairpin you have ever seen in your life. I knelt down and squeezed her with delight!

This was the first gift from my niece and the most treasured. Her excitement was in giving it. Mine was in receiving. That was more than a decade ago, but my special gift still rests in its ornate box with the shiny bow in my bedroom. It will never be tossed. It will never be used. It will always be treasured. And it didn't cost Ariana anything but the challenge of finding the right size box, and the joy of seeing her Aunt Pat receive it.

Now, don't run out and buy a package of bobby pins. Your friends and family members may not even have enough hair to swoosh back and pin. The little gift in that box was intended for me. It is a daily reminder of the simplicity of a valuable gift given with a generous heart. We can be generous, but we need to keep it simple until our debt is cleared.

When I purchased my first home in Atlanta, I hosted a house warming gathering. Friends and family members were quite generous. I suppose it was partly because I was single and they knew that funds were tight. I received fluffy towels, decorative accessories, and an array of items for the kitchen. I still have the set of Pyrex® mixing bowls that my friend Johnnie gave me. You'll never guess the most unusual gift I received that day: a package of paper towels. I kid you not! I first thought it was a joke. Thank God I didn't laugh in the giver's face. I accepted it graciously. It wasn't something warm and fuzzy. It wasn't even a name-brand package. It was a practical gift from a practical person. I was ever so grateful two weeks later when I needed one of those handy dandy off-brand towels.

Aren't you ready to ratchet down your gifting a notch or two? I already see the signs of gifting burnout. Today, it's not the carefully thought-through process that I saw in my Mom's day at Christmastime, when we'd make our way to *C.F. Lauterbach's* on Sycamore Street. (Yes, it's the same street where the doll was torn from the clutches of my bosom, leaving me in a puddle of tears.) Mom would peruse the aisles, looking for the perfect piece of crystal or china dish for her friends. The store even gift-wrapped for free! That was the 1960's. We do gifting a little differently today. At Christmastime, we make our selections from the five-pound Thanksgiving Day newspaper, choosing whatever has the biggest discount. During the year we're swayed by the commercials that pop up most frequently on television. Cookies latch onto our electronic devices, invading our space, and dropping hints of where we should turn our affections and swipe our credit cards. And if credit is a problem, there's always a six-month *same-as-cash* deal. Madison Avenue has covered all the bases, haven't they?

The countless aisles with ceiling-to-floor choices have begun to take its toll on us, financially and otherwise. In fact, physician Dr. Richard Swenson alluded to the potential adverse effects in his best sellers, *Margin* and *The Overload Syndrome*. One modern-day solution to endless gift-shopping has been the purchase of gift cards. It's fast, it's simple, and cards are everywhere. Yet, it's been reported that $1 billion in these plastic gifts go unused every year. So there goes your hard-earned money, stuffed in the recipient's drawer or between their sofa cushions, never to be redeemed.[29]

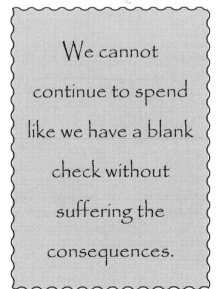

We cannot continue to spend like we have a blank check without suffering the consequences.

We can't control whether a gift card is ever used, but we *can* control how much cash stays in our wallets (not to mention the debit and credit cards). There is no simple answer to resolving the challenges in this category. Shopping is emotional. Shopping for gifts is even more emotional. But we cannot continue to spend like we have a blank check without suffering the consequences. The clock is ticking. Your precious income truly is your largest wealth-producing asset.

You will either continue to dole it out, let millions slip through your fingers over a lifetime, and become a middle-class pauper, or you will tell yourself the same thing that the little toddler heard on Sycamore Street so many years ago: *No.*

So, vow to relinquish your *shop-i-fide* crown; stick your credit cards in the freezer (if not the shredder); and start making less purchases with less money that yields the most joy in the life of the recipient, even those you happen to gift to yourself.

GIFTS and SHOPPING GALORE SAVINGS

$ _____ Buy greeting cards at a dollar store.

$ _____ Regift a gift given to you.

$ _____ Regift again! (How many candles and vases can one person have in their house?)

$ _____ Shop for Christmas by October instead of in December.

$ _____ Order flowers in the recipient's town versus paying a national online florist's surcharge.

$ _____ If ordering flowers in town, deliver them yourself!

$ _____ Set a Christmas spending budget in January, and don't go over it.

$ _____ Make a free birthday *call*, instead of sending someone a birthday card.

$ _____ Pick up the phone and call, instead of sending a Christmas card. For years, I looked forward to receiving an audible card from my former coworker and friend, Freddie.

$ _____ Call instead of sending an anniversary card.

$ _____ Call instead of sending a sympathy card. Better yet, go by in person!

$ _____ Reuse gift bags.

$ _____ Reuse gift boxes.

$ _____ Reuse wrapping paper.

$ _____ Reuse gift bows.

$ _____ Keep a spare generic gift on hand to avoid last-minute expense purchases.

$ _____ Give used books as gifts to avid readers.

$ _____ Use wallpaper for gift wrap.

$ _____ Buy gift baskets from thrift stores.

$ _____ Spend the day shopping for quality gifts at yard sales.

$ _____ Bake something vs. buying a gift.

$ _____ Buy white tissue paper vs. colored paper.

$ _____ Don't include a store card with your gift. Include a personal note, a written note!

$ _____ Finish Christmas shopping on Halloween vs. buying candy.

$ _____ Speaking of Halloween, skip the costume party.

$ _____ Call to congratulate a retiree instead of sending a retirement card.

$ _____ Wedding gift – a potted plant. (But be sure to tell the recipient *not* to water it in the shower!)

$ _____ Redeeming gift cards? Take the card and only $5 into the store. Otherwise, you'll end up buying more than the "free" card is worth!

$ _____ Reuse tissue paper – iron it smooth on the cool temperature!

$ _____ Use paper/plastic tablecloths to wrap large gifts.

$ _____ Bridal shower gift – don't buy expensive lingerie; instead, buy a large soft towel and attach a satin rose as a "teddy."

$ _____ Christmas giving – list people and the amount you will spend.

$ _____ Pay cash for Christmas gifts. **No exceptions!**

$ _____ Check wedding registries early and select a less expensive item.

$ _____ Check baby registries early and select one of the lesser expensive items to purchase.

$ _____ Your Idea - _____.

$ _____ Your Idea - _____.

$ _____ Your Idea - _____.

$ _____ TOTAL ANNUAL SAVINGS

> The less exposure to advertising, the less enticement towards shopping. Turn off the enticement leeches.

· SIXTEEN ·

Technology and Electronics: *"Louder"*

My husband will gladly disqualify me from writing a chapter on technology and electronics. After all, you're reading the words from someone who, in 2012, still had a cellphone with an antenna and valued her car's cassette player more than the CD player. Granted, I may be one of a handful of baby boomers who went kicking and screaming into the 21st century, fighting the avalanche of technological toys. I detest the portrayal of all electronic gadgets as being critical in the here and now. (How quickly we forget the 8-track and portable cassette player.) Bigger and better versions are geared towards dissolving our contentment, heightening our level of enjoyment, and multiplying our productivity, right? I'll admit, the computers *have* come a long way since they were first ushered into our homes. Now they are smaller and lighter. Monitors have followed the same pattern. Now they're both in our back pockets. I wonder where they'll end up next.

> Never buy the newest version of any device – that alone should finance your child's freshman year in college!

The frenzy to keep up with the technology-driven *Joneses* will wipe out your future nest egg in the twinkling of an eye. For the average American, what will it hurt to wait 1/8 of a second longer to have that website pop up on your flat screen? What does the premium computer speed *really* mean, and who can measure it anyway? Only the internet companies, the ones who are selling them. Why not slow down, loosen your grip on that mouse, and let some oxygen get to your brain. (Oh, that's right. Most folks have ditched their standard mouse for a flat surface version. My 20th century habits have surfaced again.) Well, you'll be glad to know that I was recently catapulted into the new world of electronics, thanks to a friend.

The Artificial Presence
My friend Karen agreed to host an 80th birthday celebration at her home for her friend and my spiritual mom, Jimmie Jones. To add humor to the special event, I composed some personal lyrics to the tune of a famous 60's hit. My new and improved cellphone (one without an antenna) would not provide ample

volume for our karaoke performance, so Karen agreed to use *her* amplification system, whatever that meant. She simply needed the karaoke website texted to her and she would take it from there.

Upon arriving at her home, she was ready to spring into action. That's when the unexpected monologue mayhem began (The artificial intelligence device's name has been changed to protect its IQ): "Stella, level four…" *Who was she talking to? We were the only ones in the room.* She repeated her command. At that moment, I saw the sleek, dome-shaped device on her kitchen bar light up. She was speaking to that inanimate object with authority, and it had a name, a *woman's* name! But Stella wasn't complying. Karen again spoke clearly and succinctly, but Stella wasn't swayed by my friend's verbal directives. She then took her commands off script: "Louder!" You had to be there to enjoy this heated monologue. Watching my highly composed friend become unglued by noncompliance from a pile of plastic and wires was quite hilarious. Needless to say, Stella never got loud enough to project our much-needed background tune, I pulled out my antiquated 20th century speaker and microphone combo, and the song went off without a hitch… and poor Stella wasn't yelled at anymore.

Can we talk plainly about this matter? Your phone may not be the most updated version, but if it presently suits your needs keep it until the battery dies! And in terms of bundled offers, perhaps some of these services may need to be unwrapped. Don't you think it's time to start doing some serious comparison shopping instead of relying upon the advice of some guy in a cubicle four states away? He's a *salesman*; he's paid to take your money, and lots of it. You don't need a device to hold six thousand photos of your toddler's first steps, or to be able to shoot a video of your elder son's third birthday party at the grand amusement park. If the truth be told, aren't we all getting a bit dizzy, watching well-meaning cohorts whisk through cellphone photos at record speed? Pictures weren't made to slide, they were made to be held and admired. Let's get a grip on this, or those hard-earned retirement dollars will keep sliding right out of our wallets.

> Do you still use a CD player, stylus, or Blackberry®? Extinction is the name of the game. Don't let your finances become extinct!

My list of items in this category is meager, to say the least. Devices come and go so quickly, so you decide what's worth your future. Even one of my original category entries became obsolete during the penning of this book. Who owns a Blackberry® anymore? Case in point.

TECHNOLOGY and ELECTRONICS SAVINGS

$ _____ Buy a smaller computer.

$ _____ Save information on your hard drive versus printing it out.

$ _____ Bypass the purchase of insurance on a cellphone and all electronic devices. My 2002 phone purchase was supposed to come with a $5/month insurance fee. Apparently, the salesman left it off my two-year contract and his "error" saved me $120.

$ _____ Determine the best way to extend the life of your phone's battery. I was told that there will be no more battery replacements, only *phone* replacements.

$ _____ Give kids prepaid phones to teach them limits.

$ _____ Get yourself a pre-paid phone.

$ _____ Buy refurbished electronic devices.

$ _____ Bundle services, only if you are willing to unbundle them after the contract period ends and the prices increase.

$ _____ Never buy the newest version of any device. (That alone should finance your child's freshman year in college!)

$ _____ Eliminate one room's much-needed television.

$ _____ Don't buy extended warranties.

$ _____ Don't buy gadgets that help you find your keys.

$ _____ Keep a wired device. A mouse that plugs into your computer doesn't need a battery!

$ _____ Your Idea: _____.

$ _____ Your Idea: _____.

$ _____ Your Idea: _____.

$ _____ TOTAL ANNUAL SAVINGS

· SEVENTEEN ·

Education: *Pomp - A Costly Circumstance*

Growing up, I thought my elementary school experience was the norm. Matoaca Laboratory School was situated on the campus of Virginia State University (formerly "College"), one of America's prestigious Historically Black Colleges. My parents worked there, so it was great to be able to ride with them to work each morning and hang out in my Dad's office before taking the 50-yard walk from Owens Hall to school.

Our building held four huge classrooms and a quaint little library located directly across from the office of our principal, Mrs. Cooper. She kept a paddle on her wall! No, I never got swatted, but there was a rumor that Alice Dodson did! We had a set of bathrooms for boys and girls. Besides a few storage closets and a restroom for staff, that was the extent of the rooms upstairs. Given the fact that it housed grades one-through-six, somebody was pretty creative when they decided that fourth and fifth graders would be taught in the same classroom, and third graders would be housed downstairs in the cafeteria! I still remember my third-grade year, having to pack up my belongings each day before the kids came through to get their trays and stroll through the lunch line, receiving a hot meal made from scratch, under the supervision of Mrs.West. She wore an oversized hairnet and dressed in all white like a nurse. The heels on her nurse-style shoes were always worn on the outer heels as if she had been standing in them for ages. Yes, all 100 of us fit inside that little building, somehow withstanding the aroma of cornbread and fried chicken between study time. Yum!

Upstairs between the classrooms were observation rooms. We students always knew that any adult at any given time could be watching us. We got pretty good at detecting the slightest of shadows moving behind the one-way mirrors, so that was our signal to sit up and pay extra attention. It never crossed my mind as a child, but our education was funded by the state, being that VSC was a state school.

High school was only a few miles away. It bore the same name as my primary school, Matoaca, named after the local Native American tribe from centuries before. It was a public institution as well, so my parents' tax dollars were still at work, educating their four children.

Tassel-Flipping Time

In 1972, the talk in our home around the subject of education began to shift. We kids had heard throughout our lives that college would follow after high school, so that was never up for discussion. But 1972 was the year that my oldest brother, Irving, enrolled at a small junior college nestled in the Blue Ridge Mountains of southwest Virginia. Mom and Dad started to have conversations about tuition, books, and housing costs. Within two years, the talks intensified. My second oldest brother Doug enrolled at Michigan State, Dad's alma mater, out of state… way out of state. I began to hear the dialogue over in-state versus out-of-state tuition, and the goal to achieve residency as quickly as possible. By 1975, education talk was in full throttle after I walked across the high school auditorium stage and flipped my tassel. Two months later, I was headed to Virginia Commonwealth University in Richmond, twenty miles from home.

By now, you have probably done the math and concluded that Mr. & Mrs. Peoples were footing the bill for three college enrollees. Irving had transferred to an in-state private four-year school, Doug was still in Michigan, and I was having the urban experience. My parents must have felt squeezed to the max, because my Dad tried everything he could to convince me to stay at home and attend Virginia State. He even offered to buy me a cute late-model compact car that later became saddled with lawsuits due to rear-end accident fires! Can you imagine a highly-respected, church-going college professor trying to bribe his daughter with such a dangerous toy! Poor Daddy; he didn't know the risks. He was just trying to keep his financial head afloat!

We didn't have much success in receiving financial aid in the form of scholarships. We were all good students but not outstanding. I did get inducted into the honor society during my senior year, but that only translated into one meager $300 scholarship from a school auxiliary and another $300 from a state funding source. It wasn't much, but it was just enough to convince my parents to let their little girl travel 20 minutes up I-95 to the state university. It turns out that in the second semester, when I visited the financial aid office to secure my second $300, they informed me that I never should have gotten it the *first* semester! We never know why things happen, but in this case, it paved the way for my entrance to the big school! Three-hundred dollars per semester sounds like a drop in the bucket compared to today's costs. It wouldn't pay for much more than a couple of textbooks. In fact, a recent internet search revealed that the books and other miscellaneous expenses at my alma mater *alone* cost more than my *entire* freshman year expenses!

Three of us siblings extended our college careers from four to five years for a variety of reasons. This piled on more unexpected costs for my parents. They carried the majority of the financial burden. Federally-funded financial aid was never an option. My parents were told repeatedly that they made too much money. *Really? State employees?*

It wasn't until after I finished my degree and began working, that I saw the enormity of college debt up close. It wasn't presented as such. In fact, the title on the paper was, "Financial Package." Who doesn't love a package? Good things come in packages, right? It seemed to excite those of us in the Peoples household that day when brother Doug got the acceptance letter from a prestigious university's school of dentistry. The annual cost was completely covered! All he had to do was show up and do the work. As we gathered in the family room to celebrate this academic milestone, I scanned the breakdown of the package deal. It's been over forty years since that day, but I still remember holding that paper and having a mind-boggling moment. I did the calculations and realized that $4000 per year was in the form of scholarships, but *$10,000* per year was from loans! And what do loans do? They rise with interest! At that point, my elation began to deflate and my concern began to grow.

Debt has a way of mushrooming. Perhaps it was college debt that single-handedly transformed such a sweet little noun like *mushroom* into a verb. Mushroom as a noun is food. We ingest it and it helps to sustain life. Mushroom as a verb doesn't instill life, especially when it's mixed with compounding interest. It makes for a disastrous duo.

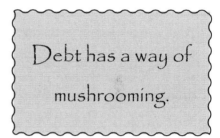

Debt has a way of mushrooming.

I won't bother sharing the Peoples college debt outcome. You probably have your own mushroom story. Financially speaking, debt mushrooms don't wither; they just mushroom. They divide and multiply like cancer. They will pull you under! They will pull your *family* under. They will tarnish any chance of building wealth for the Golden Years. I'm not making this stuff up. I've talked with parents who were struggling with meeting basic monthly obligations, only to succumb to the pull of **private** college choices with exorbitant tuition costs for their kids. *Excuse me? Did I miss something?*

I don't have any biological children. By the time I was married, my step children were grown and living on their own, earning steady incomes. I have not personally had to make hard decisions regarding kids and tuition. I have, however, been faced with the challenge of selecting the best school for graduate work. I did the research, weighed the options, and elected to enroll at an out-of-state university. Hard to believe, right? I'm the savvy snowflake trying to help you start yours rolling. How could I do such a thing? Simple; I paid as I went, one or two courses per semester. It was an external degree program, so I completed most coursework in the comfort of my den. I took advantage of reduced tuition offers. The most blessed thing happened when I was about to enroll in the last two classes. I retrieved a huge black envelope from the mailbox. The first words in the letter were, "How would you like to take two classes for the price of one?" It was hallelujah time in my house! My pay-as-you-go approach took years, but I could proudly walk across the stage at Liberty University in Virginia, not having to think about a financial Alcatraz pulling at my purse-strings.

Higher education, middle-class incomes, and $40,000 per year tuitions do **not** add up, no matter *what* type of calculator you use! This is the conversation I recently had with a friend. Her daughter was contemplating going to a well-known university in Atlanta. My friend informed me of the overly-inflated tuition. Given the fact that this rising high school senior had a part-time job and a paid-for car, and had struck up a deal to have Mom pay for her prom gown while she handled all the other prom expenses, I would have also assumed that she had done the math on college costs. I would have also assumed that she could see that considering this college choice was like considering the purchase of the Taj Mahal on a bus driver's budget. I'm happy to report that the daughter chose a state university which is almost 1/3 the cost of the Taj Mahal!

Real Life with Play Money

Do you remember a family sitcom when the father gave his son a quick lesson on economics? *Teddy* had an undiagnosed learning disability, made terrible grades in high school, and announced that he wasn't going to college. Quite naturally, *Dr. Huck* informed him that he would not be living at home so he would have to find a job. Teddy proudly said that he could easily make $1200 a month on his own. At that point, Dr. Huck spotted the Monopoly® game lying on the desk and dished out the cash to his son. They jockeyed back and forth with the fake money, with the Doc pushing the realities of life in his son's face and the son countering with ways to keep his money. I love the part when Teddy was left holding $200, gleaming from ear to ear, until his dad asked him if he planned to have a girlfriend. There went the two-hundred bucks!

If you have a child in middle school or higher, get out the fake money and play the game! Better yet, use real money. That'll really excite them! Order a pizza or two. Invite a few of their friends. Even invite their friends' parents, especially if you know they need a wake-up call as well. (Beware; you'll be exposing your monthly income, so be careful who you invite!) Print out a budget sheet. I highly recommend the one from Dave Ramsey's website.[30] It includes a space for practically every area of spending known to man. It will help you and your child see that it's the forgotten things that eat away at a budget.

Life is No Game

If you have enough money in your checking or savings account that equates to a month's gross income, withdraw it in large and small bills. Make sure you have lots of ones. Lay it out before your child and their friends, and watch their faces light up. Have last month's bills ready, as well as semi-annual and annual bills, such as insurance costs and property taxes. Decide ahead of time how you want the game to end. Do you reward your child with a certain percentage of any leftover funds? Do you give them a set amount just for playing? Do you promise them half of every utility cost that's slashed the following month? You decide what the prize will be. Whatever you choose, it will open your child's eyes to the reality of **limited funds for unlimited college expenses**.

Begin at the top: the gross income. Ask them for the amount that you give to your church or synagogue or other charitable organizations. Next, watch their eyes when you ask for the dollars to pay taxes. Refrain from smiling when you demand hundreds for gas, electric, water, and trash pick-up. Do your best not to snicker when another stack of Ben Franklin's leave their hands for groceries. Make a separate request for eating out expenses. To hammer it home, multiply one can of soda x 30 to show the monthly cost of sweet drinks. Help them unbundle their quickly-dwindling stash when you demand the alleged affordable rate for bundled internet, phone, and cable services. Don't forget to ask them the cost of their last clothing purchase and retrieve that amount from their clutches.

By now, they will probably be like Teddy, bragging about the heaping surplus that remains in their sweaty little palms. Give them a little smile. Then unload the remaining double-barrel: car payments, car insurance, car washes, oil changes, health insurance, doctor's appointments, prescriptions, cheerleader outfits, gymnastics practice, class trips, braces, and eyeglasses. If you have a pet, include all of Fido's and Chelsea's costs as well. Don't leave any stone unturned. You can't! When bills come rolling your way, they must be uncovered and dealt with. It's time to show young people the truth. If not now, when? Parents are to prepare them for life! They cannot experience life if they have their heads stuck in the sand, pretending that "life is good" while their leased car just got towed. (Or was that *your* car?)

If there is not an extra $40,000 in your budget, there is no reason for your child to be considering a college with that price tag! It doesn't matter if the head cheerleader or the football captain or Junior's best friend from grade school is going there. They don't have to pay your child's bills! Sticking a second-mortgage on your personal residence is dumb too! If you couldn't save the money *before* college, how are you ever going to pay it while they're *in* college? And don't for a minute believe that they are going to pay you back when they get out. Finally, whatever you do, don't allow them to go crawling to their *grandparents*. I could write another book about the heartbreak of grandkids fleecing their soft-hearted grands.

I can hear you saying, "I'll help them by **co-signing** their loans." Excuse me! Are you having a senior moment? Cosign a loan for an unemployed child who's getting ready to fly the coop and have the thrill of a lifetime? One whose main goal is deciding how to decorate his or her quad apartment on campus, or who shops online between classes on the latest smart phone? That wouldn't be very smart in my opinion! Even King Solomon, the wisest man on earth, said co-signing is anything *but* wise (Proverbs 22:26). And you *do* want to rear wise children, don't you? Strapping a college student to a quarter-of-a million dollars debt, or any debt, is setting them up for disaster. These are strong words, but this whole issue of

> Strapping a college student to a quarter-of-a million dollars debt, or any debt, is setting them up for disaster.

debt is pretty strong, and financial ruin sometimes causes people to resort to taking their lives. Just read about the Great Depression. I guess you could say debt is our *modern-day* Depression. There are alternatives to massive college debt. They may not be pretty to you. They may even be upsetting to the little princess who wants to attend the university with the manicured lawn or hardwood-floor dorm rooms. Junior may want to dash to the closest top-division college campus in hopes of bettering his chances at making it to the Pros. We all know that if he were *that* good, the universities would have been courting *him*! Keep the ultimate educational goal in mind: to pursue a degree that aligns with your child's talents and abilities, and that is capable of producing a viable income for life. (Spending $100,000 for a social services degree doesn't add up. You can get it for much less and still help people.)

Help your child see the long-term value of living at home while pursuing a degree. If you can, reward them with an extravagant trip each year for making the wise choice of living at home, versus spending tens of thousands at an academic bed-and-breakfast. The bottom line is this: your child's strengths and abilities may dictate their college major, but your **income** dictates the college choice. Don't fall for the finger-pointing guilt game that youngsters have mastered. The budget speaks. They can scream and yell at it all they want. Invite them to join you in making the education cost fit into the budgetary puzzle. But don't be too hard on them. In fact, before the budget exercise begins, let them order the pizza with all of their choice toppings. Besides, after the game, it may be the last major choice they make for a long time!

> The bottom line is this: your child's strengths and abilities may dictate their college major, but your income dictates the college choice.

SLASHING EDUCATIONAL COSTS

$ _____ Go to school online, if more economical.

$ _____ Go to in-state colleges.

$ _____ Choose a trade school.

$ _____ Pay cash for classes.

$ _____ Work an extra job or two to pay cash.

$ _____ Ask if there's a discount for a certain number of classes. (Remember, my last two graduate school classes were a 2-for-1 deal!)

$ _____ Buy used textbooks if they haven't been revised.

$ _____ Sell textbooks, but not on-campus. Not a very good return.

$ _____ Tutor someone.

$ _____ If you need tutoring, negotiate the price down, if 2 or more of you are being tutored.

$ _____ Buy tax-free eligible school items on your state's tax-holiday.

$ _____ Pursue an education where parents receive a discount (primary, secondary, or college.)

$ _____ Buy used uniforms.

$ _____ Sell extra uniforms.

$ _____ If possible, select a public school with uniforms to avoid excessive clothing purchases.

$ _____ In college, find the cheapest but safest housing? That could be a family's in-law suite.

$ _____ Consider pursuing a career from a trade school. I keep hearing there's a shortage in the workforce. (After all, when you need a plumber, there is no substitute!)

$ _____ Don't fall for the bait-n-switch approach of accepting a freshman scholarship, only to fork over tens of thousands the next 3 years. I know someone who experienced this.

$ _____ See if your parents' alma mater will offer a discount.

$ _____ Find a work-study program.

$ _____   Homeschool your kids before college.

$ _____   Enroll your kids in a homeschooling co-op.

$ _____   Your Idea - _____.

$ _____   Your Idea - _____.

$ _____   Your Idea - _____.

$ _____   TOTAL ANNUAL SAVINGS

Don't fall for the scholarly "bait and switch" where your child receives 100% costs their freshman year and little or nothing for the remainder. It's either 4-years or no years!

· EIGHTEEN ·

Sickness and Wellness: *Bed Pan or Panning for Gold*

This may sound crazy, but in grade school, I loved spelling tests. Maybe it's because I'm a visual learner. Stringing those characters in the right order almost always landed me a perfect score on Fridays. Applying rules like *I before E except after C*, and the vowels of the alphabet are *A, E, I, O, and U, and sometimes Y and W* guaranteed a 100 almost every time. I haven't heard those rules recited in decades. Maybe we ought to reinstitute them, instead of leaving it to young inquiring minds to "figure out" the correct spelling of words.

One of my teachers' favorite games to help expand our vocabularies involved antonyms, homonyms, and synonyms. My favorite was always antonyms. The opposites. They were so concrete. Black and white contrasts with no fuzzy gray areas. You knew where you stood. In or out, up or down, here or there. Bring on the antonyms.

The term "health care" can be viewed as a combination of two antonyms. If you have your health, you usually don't need someone to care for you. Good health equals less care, or no care at all. Let's stretch it a bit further. What if we assume that "health care" pertains to caring for a state of healthiness? What would be the antonym to that? I'd like to borrow a term that many health-conscious people are using: "sick care."

Whether Washington, the Media, your family doctor, or you own up to it or not, America is in a serious sick-care crisis. Even while I'm penning this book, Congress is seesawing over the health costs of Americans and who needs to fund them. We all can agree that medical costs have gone through the roof with no end in sight. Employers are forced to make hard decisions about supplementing the health benefits of their employees, while the average worker is left deciding whether that late-night spiked fever really warrants a visit to the emergency room. To offset sky-rocketing costs, folks who suddenly take ill are now opting to call Uber® instead of 911!

In Sickness or in Wealth

I am not going to belabor the point. We all have an opinion on what's broken with our system. In my opinion, co-payments have done us all a disservice. The ease of paying $35 for a doctor's visit and another $20 for a prescription has caused us *all* to become lazy in not only improving our health but striving for wellness. Did I just say that out loud? Do I need to say it again? We are downright **lazy**. And sad to say, this mindset has spilled over into our spending habits.

What would you do if you were told that in two years your health insurance premium would double, your co-payment would triple, and you would pay full retail for all prescriptions? How would you change your approach to wellness? Or would it change? I have actually seen this happen in the lives of many Americans over the last few years. Many have even been forced to buy health coverage that they didn't want (or be monetarily penalized.) Sounds like a tax to me!

While Congress debates the extent of their role in dispensing your sick care, why not do everything you can to take control of your own health, and at the same time save your money towards retirement? Start looking in your cupboards to see what hidden gems you might have to help withstand the rising tide of medical costs, rather than hoping for more free samples from your doctor. Some of grandma's home remedies may work after all. They may sound antiquated, but some of them must have worked; she lived to be a grandma! I'm not advocating for the return of the 1950's medicine cabinet contents.

I grew up watching Mom and Dad reach for band-aids, aspirins, and mercurochrome®. This antiseptic came in a teeny tiny glass bottle and could kill any germ within a foot of it (if we survived the sting first!) Later, the pink stuff for upset digestive systems came along. It looked yummy, but one swallow changed our minds. To alleviate bug bites, we covered ourselves with good ol' calamine lotion. It had a distinct aroma that you could never forget. For any breathing and stuffiness issues, Mom would dip her finger into the jar of a translucent substance and smear it over our chests and underneath our noses. Mom had one last piece of arsenal in her cupboard for upset stomachs. I don't recall the name of it, but the impact will forever be on my taste buds. It reminded me of a cross between a pine-scented cleaner and turpentine. Did your Mom have some too?

In 2016, Genworth, one of America's largest insurance companies, released some staggering figures. They reported that the cost of a private nursing home room was almost *double* the cost of home health care. Costs vary, and are dependent upon the state in which you reside. For example, in my current state of Georgia, one could expect to pay over $41,000 annually for home health care, versus over $74,000 for a private nursing home room.[31]

These numbers even overwhelmed me! I thought that my Dad's 2008 nursing home costs of $50,000 would have taken 15 to 20 years to double. How wrong I was! However, it looks as if my retirement estimation of $1 million per couple may not be that far-fetched. Given the statistics by many insurers that the average person has a 2 ½ year stint in some form of assisted living, coupled with a projected 4% increase per year, annual costs by 2026 may top $110,000! (Sounds like college tuition costs, huh?) And this doesn't include any special amenities like the ones I mentioned earlier for my Dad: the seat cushion to redistribute his weight, or a customized mattress, not covered by Medicare, but allegedly designed to prevent bedsores…we won't even go there. Daddy's initial monthly costs hovered around $4,500 but topped out well over $5,000. In retrospect, wouldn't long term care insurance have made a huge difference? Absolutely! It helps to gather all the pieces of the financial picture, folks. Do it while you can.

So why all the talk about nursing homes in a chapter that purports health, wellness, and well-being? Because usually it's not until we're jarred with real numbers that we decide to make drastic changes for the sake of wellness. Rising premiums don't lie. Rising prescription costs don't lie. Don't be hoodwinked into thinking that all of your future antibiotic needs will fall under the umbrella of a few "free" selected drugs offered by your local pharmacist. The industry could not sustain itself if a large percentage of medication costs were not passed onto the consumer. (Nor could they afford to pay out dividends to their shareholders.)

So, my debt-busting friends, would you not agree that it pays to get healthy and *stay* healthy as long as you can? It may serve us well to revisit some of those annoying statements from our elders; statements like, "eat an apple a day;" "down your chicken soup;" "eat your spinach;" "drink more water;" "go to bed;" and "take in some fresh air." From my point of view, these phrases beat hearing the words, "Mrs. Smith, time to take your pills," *any* day.

> We can't go wrong with walking, water, and way more vegetables!

SICKNESS and WELLNESS SAVINGS

$ _____   Increase your health insurance deductible.

$ _____   Wear a mask when cutting the grass to help ward off respiratory issues.

$ _____   Open windows/doors in the winter to let out cold and other virus germs.

$ _____   Get a second opinion regarding dental work.

$ _____   If you smoke, smoke one less cigarette daily.

$ _____   Disinfect hotel rooms.

$ _____   Keep hands away from your face (to decrease acne and contact with germs.)

$ _____   Periodically clean off surfaces with sanitizers (office, home, car.)

$ _____   Keep your purse off floors to avoid spreading germs.

$ _____   Never wrap partials/dentures in napkins. They may get tossed.

$ _____   Floss to help minimize cavities and gum disease. (A tip from my brother the dentist.)

$ _____   Eat oatmeal to help reduce cholesterol.

$ _____   Buy gym equipment at the thrift store or a secondhand exercise equipment store.

$ _____   Don't go in the sun without sunscreen.

$ _____   Take nutrition, preferably a liquid form for better absorption. (Thank you Reliv International, Inc. You've been providing this great product internationally for over 30 years!)

$ _____   Keep sanitizer in your car and purse.

$ _____   Change your toothbrush frequently.

$ _____   Choose a place where you can park a little farther away and walk.

$ _____   Don't skimp on your daily nutritional regimen. It'll cost you in the long-run. (My Reliv supplements have helped to boost my immune system for the past 17 years, thus easing symptoms from colds, flus, and a whole lot more from head to toe!)

$ _____   Eat more fiber for better digestion and decreased need for antacids.

$ _____   Price medications; buy online if possible after consulting your doctor.

$ _____ Price generic medication brands and consult your doctor.

$ _____ Get second and third opinions on major surgical procedures.

$ _____ Transfer prescriptions to another pharmacy with a lower rate.

$ _____ Transfer prescriptions to another pharmacy that offers a store gift card.

$ _____ Review medical bills for errors.

$ _____ No private hospital room!

$ _____ See if a surgical procedure can be done in the doctor's office versus a more expensive setting such as the hospital.

$ _____ Your Idea - _____.

$ _____ Your Idea - _____.

$ _____ Your Idea - _____.

$ _____ TOTAL ANNUAL SAVINGS

· NINETEEN ·

Travel: *Dips and Dives*

The travel experience has changed quite a bit over the last few decades. We've all felt it at the airport, from taking snail steps through long security lines to having to say goodbye to loved ones at the entrance to the concourse. I remember in the early 80's when my Mom got to the airport, only to discover she had left her driver's license at home. She didn't panic but presented the next best valid ID: her JC Penney® credit card! Can you imagine that? Don't ask me how, but they let her board that plane! It must have been her honest looking face. Today she would be laughed out of the terminal.

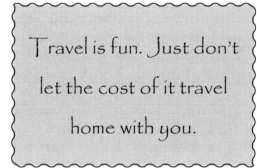

Travel is fun. Just don't let the cost of it travel home with you.

The adventures of flying deserve a book all to themselves. I choose to fly only to reach my destination quickly, not because I relish the thought of breaking the sound barrier. When I'm up, up, and away, I don't mind being shaken side-to-side, like in an amusement park's bumpy car. But please, oh please, don't dip me. Dipping is more torturous than fingernails on a chalkboard. It resembles drops on a roller-coaster. Did I mention I abhor rollercoasters? I can live without having my mind bent or screaming at the top of my lungs on a spine-twisting machine. *Shakin'* is in, but *dippin'* is **out**.

When I board a plane, I try to ignore the inevitable. I take my seat and tighten my belt one tug away from cutting off my circulation. When we start to taxi down the runway, I skim every magazine within reach. I tune into the flight attendant outlining the cabin rules and safety procedures. And when the plane lifts off, I ask myself, *what are you doing in here*? I pray when we're going up and I pray when we're coming down. But, oh boy, when we dip, I freak. Not outwardly, but inwardly. Every cell in my body from head to toe is screaming, *get me out of here*! I look poised and polished on the outside. But if you took a closer look, you'd see my body chemistry being altered, and my pupils dilating like *The Incredible Hulk*®, minus the green tint. Plane rides can accelerate anybody's prayer life like nothing else.

Rockin' Over the Rockies

I don't have time to tell you about the trip to Reno. Then again, maybe I do. The young flight attendant had said there were no worries. I had my doubts. The jet was fast but it was small, very small. We had to bend down to climb into our seats. The first hour was just as she said. I'll give her credit for that. She gets an F on the last 20 minutes. It was a living nightmare. Strong, male frequent flyers began to voice "whoas" and "wows." Even the arrogant businessman seated next to me clutched his handle and blurted out, "*that was a big one!*" Did I need him to tell me that? I told you I don't like dips! Only this wasn't a dip. It was a drop, one after another after another. There we were, bouncing over the Rocky Mountains, dipping and dropping and dipping and dropping. I don't like *dippin'*! And *droppin'* ain't up my alley either!

And what about that smaller-than-life plane from Abilene, Texas? It would have been better to have made the two-hour drive to and from Dallas. Jumping around in the air at 6:30 in the morning in a piece of aluminum resembling a crop duster is *not* a good wake-up call. Did I mention what I saw from the window? Propellers. Yes, like the ones in an original Tarzan movie. I don't like to look out windows while I'm in the air either, except when we clear the clouds. Wherever we are in the stratosphere, my seatbelt stays secure. Why? Because I don't like *dippin'*!

Cruises are another story. Ahh, the calm and serenity of it all. From the time you climb the boarding plank until the time of departure, you're treated like kings and queens. Passengers and crew are all jovial, even during the emergency drill. Who would think that a bunch of strangers huddled in packs wearing life jackets could have such a blast!

When you finally reach your cabin, no one cares that it's the size of a kitchen pantry from the 50's, and if you're lucky, you have one peephole. Once you store your belongings in the shoebox closet and head out the door, you're hit with one thrill after another. The lights, the noise, and the attractions are in your face. Cruises have everything, except dips. Granted, a few unfortunate guests may suffer motion sickness. Believe me, they haven't felt motion until they've weathered a crop duster ride and fought the wind shear of the Rockies.

Excursions are always an extra expense, taking you to deserted islands or allowing you to swim with the dolphins. Off-Broadway shows are a treat in themselves. Duty-free shopping keeps any woman occupied for hours on end. These are all well and good, but there's nothing like the infamous buffets. If the corners of your lips just curled, you've been there. Buffets start before sunrise, with the clanking of hot trays and the chatter of rested cargo. Two hours later, the scrumptious post-breakfast edibles are rolled out. By the time you awaken from your mid-morning nap on the upper deck, lunch is calling your name. You may have just gotten acquainted with your surroundings, but lunch already knows your name. You've been introduced to breakfast, and dinner can't wait to meet you. The passenger lines quickly form, and before you know it, you're juggling a cup, a plate, and all the silverware necessary for the experience. You may accidentally drop a spoon or two, but with a few risings and settings of the sun you have the balancing act mastered.

Isn't it amazing how much peace one can experience from one paragraph to the next? Cruises have no dips. Maybe a wave or two, but no dips. You just drift into a world of utter relaxation. Pupils don't dilate and blood doesn't drain from tense knuckles. You just float, stroll, rest, and eat. Who wouldn't want that? Whether in the air or on the sea, we've got to keep tabs on our wallets. Be careful that those dollars aren't drifting out to sea while you're being financially lulled to sleep. Cruises are a great getaway, but they are still money makers for the Industry. That means they are potential money *takers* for us passengers. Don't fall for their endless schemes to invade your wallet, beginning with the welcome picture that has you standing under a cardboard palm tree. Six weeks on land and you won't even remember where you sailed, and that photo will be stuffed in a box, along with the sea shells and souvenir magnets.

Travel is fun. Just don't let the cost of it travel home with you. Set a budget and stick to it. Plan far enough in advance to avoid hasty and costly decisions. Scour the internet for all savings options. Have the cash on-hand or stay home. Remember, retirement for us baby boomers is here or right around the corner. Before you know it, you Generation Xers will be lining up for your gold watches too. You need to have something to show for your decades of hard work.

So, whether you're bound for air, land, or sea, enjoy yourself. Keep exorbitant costs at bay. In other words, do all you can to avoid dipping into retirement savings at the expense of short-term thrills. I purpose to do this with every trip. After all, I hate *dippin'*.

TRAVEL SAVINGS

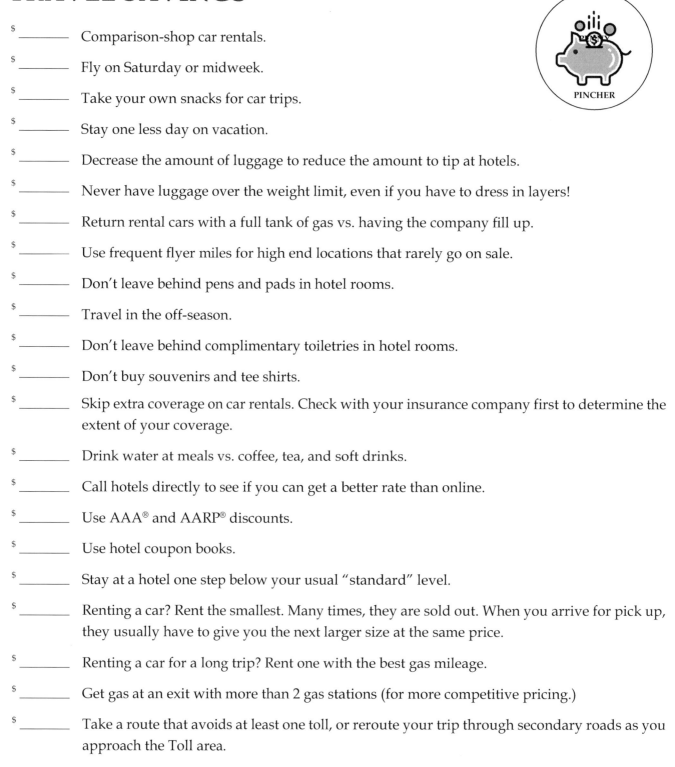

$ _____ Comparison-shop car rentals.

$ _____ Fly on Saturday or midweek.

$ _____ Take your own snacks for car trips.

$ _____ Stay one less day on vacation.

$ _____ Decrease the amount of luggage to reduce the amount to tip at hotels.

$ _____ Never have luggage over the weight limit, even if you have to dress in layers!

$ _____ Return rental cars with a full tank of gas vs. having the company fill up.

$ _____ Use frequent flyer miles for high end locations that rarely go on sale.

$ _____ Don't leave behind pens and pads in hotel rooms.

$ _____ Travel in the off-season.

$ _____ Don't leave behind complimentary toiletries in hotel rooms.

$ _____ Don't buy souvenirs and tee shirts.

$ _____ Skip extra coverage on car rentals. Check with your insurance company first to determine the extent of your coverage.

$ _____ Drink water at meals vs. coffee, tea, and soft drinks.

$ _____ Call hotels directly to see if you can get a better rate than online.

$ _____ Use AAA® and AARP® discounts.

$ _____ Use hotel coupon books.

$ _____ Stay at a hotel one step below your usual "standard" level.

$ _____ Renting a car? Rent the smallest. Many times, they are sold out. When you arrive for pick up, they usually have to give you the next larger size at the same price.

$ _____ Renting a car for a long trip? Rent one with the best gas mileage.

$ _____ Get gas at an exit with more than 2 gas stations (for more competitive pricing.)

$ _____ Take a route that avoids at least one toll, or reroute your trip through secondary roads as you approach the Toll area.

$ _____ Pack snacks in your luggage.

$ _____ No in-room movies.

$ _____ No in-room gaming.

$ _____ Don't pay extra for internet access.

$ _____ Reserve a hotel room with a micro fridge to store carry-out meals and your own food from home.

$ _____ Don't leave behind the pieces of soap that you use in the hotel room.

$ _____ Skip room service, unless it's a special occasion.

$ _____ If you have room service, choose a lesser expensive item.

$ _____ Order soup/salad vs. a full dinner for at least one meal.

$ _____ Always rent cars in advance. Walk-up prices may be much higher.

$ _____ If possible, rent a car OFF airport lots. Airports usually have a surcharge.

$ _____ Planning an extended trip including car rental, and the airport rental costs are outlandish? Take a cab to an off-airport site.

$ _____ Your Idea - _____.

$ _____ Your Idea - _____.

$ _____ Your Idea - _____.

$ _____ TOTAL ANNUAL SAVINGS

> All-inclusive and package trips may cost more. Do the math and be frugal while having fun.

· TWENTY ·

Miscellaneous: *A Penny Saved*

If you're over 50, you probably remember the singing group, the *Monkees*®. One of the singers, Michael Nesmith, had a famous mom, Bette Graham. She, undoubtedly, has touched many of our lives with her invention. Being a less-than-perfect typist, she developed paint that would hide her typographical errors. Known to us as *Liquid Paper*®, she originally referred to it as *Mistake Out*. That gooey white paint went on to land her a $47.5 million deal with the Gillette Corporation. Bette got the royalties, and we got our hands on a nifty little invention that has helped us wipe out many an error.[32] *Liquid Paper*® has served us well. It was worth its weight in gold. But not everything carries the same weight of importance. And if it doesn't serve a purpose, it doesn't need to be bought.

> If you started with one penny at the beginning of the month and doubled the total every day for 30 days, by the end of that month you would have over $5,000,000!

Do you know how you can tell whether you've squandered your hard-earned cash on stuff? Try opening your kitchen cabinet without the contents clobbering you. See if you can categorize its contents. Do you really need a gadget that stands your bacon on end? Can't old fashioned paper towels drain the grease? And why not give your bored teenager the task of flattening aluminum cans with his foot instead of buying a gadget to do it. I must admit, the pancake batter dispenser looks like a pretty handy device. The only problem is no one's cooking at home. We're all crammed into the local pancake house, paying someone else to flip our pile of dough!

My good friends, Woodrow and Chelsea, have been married almost 40 years. Woodrow is a former professional football player. During their first few years of marital bliss, money was no object. Their posh condo overlooked Atlanta's Chattahoochee River. Woodrow would sport around town in his white Alfa Romero® convertible with red interior, while Chelsea frequented her favorite boutique, Neiman Marcus®. She used to tease her husband about his giant water cooler dispenser bottle. It was filled with various coins that, in her opinion, were just in the way and another dust collector. Her teasing came to a screeching halt three years later when Woodrow abandoned football to attend Bible school and pursue full-time Christian ministry. Chelsea still recalls the night they sat with those dust-collecting coins sprawled on the kitchen table, counting stacks of one-hundred cents, just to have enough for diapers and groceries. That collection of dusty metal became a financial lifeline during lean years.

We may not all leave a six-figure income to pursue another venture, but chances are, we have all experienced periods of financial leanness. Those pennies that we walk over in the parking lot could one day come back to haunt us. This last chapter of savings is a hodgepodge of ideas to add just a few more pennies to your account. After all, a penny saved is *still* saving! And by the way, if you started with one penny at the beginning of the month and doubled the total every day for 30 days, by the end of that month you would have over $5,000,000! Ponder that, the next time you step over Lincoln's head.

> Park in infrequently parked spaces. Dropped coins are more likely to be waiting for you!

MISCELLANEOUS SAVINGS

$ _____ Sing instead of reading billboards.

$ _____ Borrow a book versus buying it.

$ _____ Save all money you didn't expect to receive.

$ _____ When someone says they can fix your problem, ask yourself, "why can't I do that?" Do it yourself.

$ _____ Get organized to avoid buying things that you already have, but can't find!

$ _____ Don't take financial advice from friends unless they are all out of debt or passionately pursuing it.

$ _____ Tell someone about this plan. If they laugh, you know they're broke and you're on the right track towards financial freedom.

$ _____ Never feed dollars into vending machines!

$ _____ Read *The Millionaire Next Door*.[33] The wealthy have a different view of money. (I heard that you can even download it for free.)

$ _____ Do one money-saving thing that your parents did and you swore you'd never do.

$ _____ If you have a storage unit, you have too much stuff! Sell something, and give the rest away.

$ _____ Don't watch television infomercials. (My past bank book can tell you about that!)

$ _____ Don't respond to radio infomercials. They are just as luring as their TV counterparts.

$ _____ Don't buy bubble packaging wrap; save it when you get packages or when store clerks and stockroom personnel are throwing it away.

$ _____ Identify the ONE thing you positively will not give up… then give it up for a month.

$ _____ Read a chapter of Proverbs daily. There's much wisdom in that book.

$ _____ Choose less pictures to have printed.

$ _____ Don't do double prints on all photos.

$ _____ Weigh the cost of renewal fees. (My profession's licensing fee costs $10 more with online credit card service versus mailing it in.)

$ _____ Buy a "must have" book at a used bookstore.

$ _____ Contact your homeowner's insurance agent to identify a way to lower your rate.

$ _____ Avoid extended warranties. They are huge money-makers for retailers.

$ _____ Say "no" to one magazine purchase.

$ _____ Mail an item parcel post vs. priority mail, even if it's a ten-cent savings.

$ _____ Ask for other's trash. (One time I made an appeal for friends' "stuff," particularly in the office and craft item categories. I received an assortment of jewels, including entire reams of copier paper!)

$ _____ Don't use vending machines unless you have the correct change.

$ _____ Think before you trash it. Can items be reused, used for another purpose, be recycled, or help someone else?

$ _____ **Continuously read this book for one year to reinforce your new saving habit.**

$ _____ Stop saying, "I need." Most modern-day needs are justified indulgences. Say "no" to something every day. We spend our terrible 2's saying "no," only to grow up to say "yes" to every whim. Grow up and say "no."

$ _____ Check bulletin boards and social media posts for free items.

$ _____ Check bulletin boards and social media posts for items you are planning to buy.

$ _____ Don't send a letter when a postcard will do.

$ _____ Share this with someone who really needs to save for their future. They may be very grateful. They may even treat you to a meal! (This happened to me. I shared my retirement journey and investment strategy with a former co-worker, and she treated me to a delicious brunch.)

$ _____ DO NOT PROCRASTINATE on financial matters. I delayed contacting a former employer about a discrepancy in my salary. The results were an overpayment that equaled the cost of a new car!

$ _____ Buy a watch battery instead of a new watch.

$ _____ Buy a watch that winds up.

$ _____ Skip a pack of gum, or tobacco, or whatever you chew!

$ _____ Forget the notion that Washington or the President will take care of you. (If no one has paid you a visit as of yet, don't expect a visit in the nursing home.)

$ _____ Chew half a piece of gum.

$ _____ Talk with banks/mortgage companies about securing the job of cleaning their foreclosed homes.

$ _____ Rent a bedroom to a college student or someone who infrequently travels to your town for business.

$ _____ Rent a bedroom to Monday-Friday commuters.

$ _____ Skip "scratch off" lottery tickets.

$ _____ Skip lottery tickets altogether.

$ _____ On the day of your birthday each month (for me, the 5th), don't buy anything other than food and gas.

$ _____ Don't buy raffle tickets.

$ _____ Grab $1 right now and stick it in a savings jar.

$ _____ If you smoke, buy cheaper cigarettes; the bad taste will make you *want* to quit!

$ _____ Thank God for one non tangible thing per day.

$ _____ Use lots of stamps? Buy a Forever Stamp® roll. (I've often wondered if they chose the name "Forever" because you can use them forever, or because they are forever going up in price!)

$ _____ Recycle glass for money.

$ _____ Write on half of a notepad and save the other half for later.

$ _____ Re-use the other side of copier paper.

$ _____ Don't ball up paper trash; tear it up to lay flat and reduce space in the trash can.

$ _____ Take the batteries out of watches that you don't wear often.

$ _____ Buy sunglasses at the dollar store.

$ _____ Planning to move? It may be cheaper to move during the week versus the weekend or the end/first part of the month.

$ _____ Moving? Decrease costs by de-cluttering, if the movers charge by the pound.

$ _____ Moving? Move some items yourself to cut the movers' hours.

$ _____ Use the "quick print" option on your printer to conserve ink.

$ _____ Store all batteries in one place to avoid buying unnecessary ones.

$ _____ Get money for referring someone to a fitness club, opening accounts, etc.

$ _____ You don't believe this will work? Develop your own plan, but do it quickly. Each month you delay costs you dearly in the long-run.

$ _____ Purchase another copy of this book directly from the author instead of Amazon®!

$ _____ Need extra income? Join a quality network-marketing company with a reputable track record that offers ongoing **free** training. (Once again, thank you Reliv International, Inc.!)

$ _____ Your Idea: _____.

$ _____ Your Idea: _____.

$ _____ Your Idea: _____.

$ _____ TOTAL ANNUAL MISCELLANEOUS SAVINGS

· TWENTY-ONE ·

Time is of the Essence

I wouldn't classify myself as a lover of science fiction, but there is one movie that I loved watching as a child: *Fantastic Voyage*. I've never heard anyone speak of it in conversation nor seen a post or comment on social media about its white-knuckling scenes. This 1966 thriller depicts a surgical team of Americans who are shrunken and injected into a scientist's blood stream. Their mission is to reach and repair an externally inoperable blood clot in his brain. They have exactly 60 minutes to get in, travel to the clot, fix it, and get out before the miniaturization wears off. The last few minutes of the film will leave you teetering on the edge of your seat![34]

When I first saw the movie, I remember the beginning as being quite boring. I happened to watch it long enough for the plot to unfold and their travel to begin. By that time, I was *hooked*! The movie's depiction of the human body's organs, intricate vascular system, and defense mechanisms captivated me the moment the team and their tiny submarine were injected into the bloodstream, and they began their journey to a designated target, not knowing what they would face along the way. They sometimes veered off course and an enemy within the group was exposed, but they were determined to fulfill their mission. (I won't tell you how it ends. It's worth watching when you need a pick-me-up.)

Your Fantastic Voyage

So, the moment has arrived. The blob is gone. You have cleared your debt. You now have a surplus in your budget that you can use to get the ball rolling. But before you make the first push, make sure that you have a *sizeable* amount in liquid accounts such as savings, CDs, and money markets (40-50% of your annual take-home pay) for huge unexpected emergencies. There's nothing worse than having to stop and restart investing due to unforeseen events and under-funded categories.

As I stated earlier in the book, I am **not** a financial advisor. I can only share my experiences with all of their bumps and bruises. The final decision in how to invest your money is totally up to you. Investing is a fluid process, so if one approach doesn't work you can always modify it to suit your needs.

> No one can predict the future...but you must be prepared for it.

One challenge I have had throughout my lifetime is finding people in the financial world who were knowledgeable and trustworthy, and offered quality advice that I could understand.

A few so-called reputable advisors have crossed my path who selected insurance and investment options that produced miniscule growth for me, while providing exorbitant commissions for themselves! I may not understand everything about the financial world, but when someone now approaches me with investment *chatter* without explanation, I head for the hills! Lack of knowledge and *understanding* has devastated my financial portfolio and melted away years of monetary growth that can never be recouped. (Remember Appendix A?)

> Investing is a fluid process, so if one approach doesn't work you can always modify it to suit your needs.

Over the last few years, my husband and I have sought counsel from a reputable investment firm in the metro Atlanta area recommended by a dear friend. After a conversation with the owner, he felt that we were quite capable of investing our funds without his assistance. (When was the last time you met anyone in the financial world who turned down an opportunity to acquire a customer?) Because of this gentleman's honesty and integrity, we have felt comfortable reaching out to his firm for periodic assistance, and their advice to us has remained the same. They have declined the opportunity to earn a commission, yet have included us in various client appreciation affairs, as well as the office's quarterly prayer time for clients. Their doors remain open in the event we decide to appoint them as managers over our financial affairs. While we have currently chosen to build our future snowball single-handedly, it's good to know that we have at least one reputable alternative waiting in the wings to give us an added push.

I recently had a lengthy conversation with a trusted friend in the financial investment and insurance world. Mark Selman explained concepts that I only knew in part, but finally made sense as a whole! He stressed key factors for selecting an advisor to manage one's financial matters:

1. Seek out references from trusted friends and professional people who have actually used their services over an extended period of time and are completely satisfied.

2. Arrange for an appointment with the reference, where you can instinctively get a feel for whether you two are a good "fit." During the appointment, seek to obtain satisfactory answers to the following questions: What is their philosophy on investing or estate planning? Do they ask questions about your long and short-term goals for the future? Do they ask about any drawbacks or

unpleasant experiences that you've had in the past (which could be potential roadblocks that you may need to overcome in order to be willing to accept their instruction?) Are they a good listener or are they in a hurry to "close the deal?" Do they give you ample time to ask your questions and make decisions, or are they irritated by your hesitancy? Do they take comprehensive notes as you (and your spouse) share your current financial position and what you hope to achieve? How they respond in these areas could be a good indicator of how they will respond in future encounters. If they don't have time for you in the beginning, don't expect it to change once they've got your automatic bank draft rolling!

3. Under no circumstances should you take anyone's opinion without making them **prove** it! When presented with an array of products, ask, "why *this* and not *that*?" "Why invest in X fund versus Y fund?" Understand how and what properly selected insurance products could be the missing link in a chain towards financial security. (My friend even shared with me a tip that the rich use to secure their wealth! I might share it with you on my Facebook page or website someday, so stay tuned!) In addition, using an advisor knowledgeable in an array of products (e.g., insurance *and* investments) will allow them to guide you in all of the pertinent avenues of wealth-building.

> The principal factor to keep in mind in all situations is to make sure that any professional who lends their advice has the heart and approach of a teacher.

4. The principal factor to keep in mind in all situations is to make sure that any professional who lends their advice has the heart and approach of a teacher. If they know their product well, they should know how to, and be willing, to convey its benefits to you without coming unglued! Those who have something wonderful to share are excited to do so with patience. Those who have something to hide are not; agreed?

Here Today, Gone Tomorrow

Investments in single stocks can be very risky. I speak from experience. Many years ago, I invested in a reputable NASDAQ®-traded company when the stocks were hovering around $6 per share. I had watched the shares climb from $2 to the $6 mark. Realizing I was losing ground, I jumped in. Things were looking up, up and away. A year later they were over $10 and poised to climb even higher. The company was rock-solid, so I increased my investment even more. The stock rose to $16 per share. Around the same time, I found myself enrolled in a stock trading seminar, eager to learn the ins and outs of trading from a "technical" position. That two-day seminar exposed me to a plethora of terms and techniques I'd never heard before. The one technique I must have missed was, "buy low and sell high." What's that old saying, "what goes up must come…" Yes, you know the rest of the story. It's been over ten years, and that stock continues to hover around $4.

I do recall one particularly unforgettable thing that happened during the seminar. The young geek who taught the class was brilliant, to say the least. He was able to whisk through technical trading methods, analyzing patterns of stock performances that the average eye would easily overlook. He explained the purpose of puts, calls, straddles, and covered calls. I thought we had entered the animal kingdom when he began making references towards bears and bulls!

When he decided to give an example of selecting a stock based upon historical performance patterns, he picked a random American company. Using technical analysis, the instructor predicted that this company should see a rise in its stock prices over the next few years. Being quite familiar with the company, I jotted a short note as a reminder to make a sizeable purchase. My investment would have likely been in the neighborhood of $3000. My note read, "Buy Apple® stock." I jotted this around 2005. That year the company's stock closed out the year a little over $10 per share. As of November 2018, it was $200 per share. I heard what the instructor said. I knew the success of the company. I wrote the note. I never **acted** on the note. Excuse me while I pound my forehead for the umpteenth time!

Gold mine single stocks are hard to spot. By the time you spot them, their price is out of reach for the average Joe. The lesson I learned with selecting single stocks is that I should never invest money that I can't afford to lose. Remember major corporation collapses in the early 2000s, resulting in scores of Americans losing their entire life-savings? Many hard-working employees had invested all of their money in their companies' stocks, and it all vanished overnight. If your newly-captured financial flakes are burning a hole in your hand and you still want to launch out into the stock trading territory, keep a very close eye on their performance!

Mutual funds have served our family well. They spread the risk and volatility of several companies, while offering more stability than single stocks. They have reasonable fees that are spelled out upfront. In choosing this investment method, the nightly news doesn't shake us to the core over one company's bankruptcy or scandal, and the sweeping of one major drug from pharmacy shelves doesn't wipe out our portfolio.

Slow and Steady

If you're in my generation, you may be feeling a bit sweaty under the collar. You know that the years ahead are fewer than the years behind. You may be asking, "How can I ever catch up? I don't have 20 years to invest." I had those same concerns a few years ago. I would listen to a financial advisor on the radio encouraging young callers to save consistently each month, and in 30 years they could see their efforts grow to over a million. It seemed pointless. Then I began to look at investing from a different perspective. This wasn't money that I would be dipping into for a car or trip or new leather couch. The budget was designed to take care of those purchases. Invested funds are to be used to meet my needs if and when I need them *later* in life. If I include future expenses for things such as cars and trips in the *monthly* budget, then the rest can be left to grow for many years!

Although our years are numbered, we don't know how many we have left, so we have to prepare for longevity. (And you know first-hand how much that runs in my family.) So, start where you are. Get the ball rolling. Who knows, it could roll for the next 20 or 30 years, compounding along the way.

The tortoise knew about a slow roll. Remember the story? The speedy hare was always bragging about how fast he could run. One day, the tortoise got tired of hearing the hare's mouth, so he challenged him to a race. The overly confidant hare took him up on the offer. All the animals in the forest gathered to see this event. The race was on! The hare took off, flying down the road and leaving the tortoise in the dust. After a while, he looked back and wasn't even able to see the tortoise anywhere in his view. Knowing he had this race in the bag, he decided to take a little nap. While the hairy rabbit laid snoring underneath a tree, the tortoise kept stepping and stepping and stepping. His perseverance caused him to step right on past the hare. The cheers from the animals were so loud that they eventually woke up the hare. He shook himself and panicked when he saw how close the tortoise was to the finish line. He took off running again at lightning speed, but it was too late. The tortoise quietly and steadily stepped across the finish line and won the race. From that day forward, the hare sadly reminded himself of an important lesson: "Don't brag about your lightning pace, for Slow and Steady won the race!"[35]

Our modern-day tortoise approach is called dollar-cost averaging. I don't understand how it works. It doesn't seem to add up. But it's a slow and steady method of consistent investing with long-term benefits. A good friend in the financial world recently defined it this way:

> Our modern-day tortoise approach is called dollar-cost averaging.

"Dollar-cost averaging is the process of investing the same amount on a periodic basis or regular intervals—monthly, quarterly, semi-annually, annually, regardless of the share price of the particular investment. When the market is up, you purchase fewer shares at the higher price; when the market is down, you purchase more shares at the lower price. The overall result is a lower average share purchase cost."[36] The end results usually exceed a racy and sporadic approach.

In my mind, I couldn't grasp how small monthly saving could exceed investing a large lump sum upfront and letting compounded interest do its job over the same time period. So, I put this concept to the test a few years ago. After Anthony and I paid off his former house, we pondered selling it versus continuing to rent it and risk another economic downturn and housing market flop. (It never really recovered, and the thought of it bottoming out again has been unthinkable.) One evening I spent some time on an investment calculate website, plugging in some numbers. I compared the potential growth in 15 years if we *sold* the house and invested the proceeds *or* invested a portion of each month's rent for 15 years at 10% growth annually. This is what I discovered:

<u>Example:</u>
Sell - $50,000 invested at 10% for 15 years = $222,695 (minus taxes)
Rent $700 per month invested at 10% for 5 years, $800 per month for the next 5 years, and $900 for the final 5 years = $321,007 (minus taxes)
The difference - **$98,312** (minus those good ole taxes)

The math is astounding, isn't it? Well, the bell has sounded. The snow is falling. The race has begun. Remember: slow and steady. The tortoise always wins.

How Much Is Enough?

I remember a relative posing a rhetorical question to me years ago. Her husband had always been a smart, level-headed guy who was quite savvy in terms of financial matters. He had made wise decisions in life, many times seeking counsel from his Dad beforehand. From an estate planning perspective, their family was on track because of smart financial planning. But in terms of overall saving, the wife asked, "How much is enough?" That's probably the number one question posed during most investment counseling sessions.[37]

Unfortunately, there is no clear-cut answer to this question. I've heard many financial advisors suggest that we need to draft a savings strategy based upon 70% of our final employment income in order to maintain our current lifestyle during retirement. Others are now questioning this estimation, proposing that it's too high of an estimation.[38]

For years I've heard people suggest that retirees will have more income because they'll be in a lower tax bracket, allowing them to bring home more. I personally disagree with this. Given the aging condition of our nation and the surmounting Medicare costs, I believe that all of our taxes will be raised to foot the bill for this industry. It's a government-run industry. *We* (believe it or not) are the government, so *we* have to fund it. In my opinion, it may not be wise to base your future financial needs on any amount less than what you are already spending.

During our last financial advisement session, Anthony and I were given a rather interesting formula for "predicting" our future financial needs. It was suggested that we total all of our projected future expenses/goals (e.g., recreation/travel, renovations, car purchases, final home purchase, charitable giving, and **long-term care** costs), determine an estimated amount of time over which these expenses might occur (or what we think might be our lifespan), determine the **annual** amount needed to cover the expenses, and then divide that amount by 12 to determine the **monthly** amount. Then, based upon our current financial savings window, determine the amount needed to cover the difference. Here is an example in round numbers:

1. For the next 25 years we project needing $1,500,000 to cover things **above** our current monthly expenses.

2. $1,500,000 divided by 25 years = $60,000 per **year** additional income

3. $60,000 divided by 12 months - = $5,000 per **month**.

4. How much is available in the current budget to offset this monthly expense? In this example, let's use **$1,000**. Suppose a $1,000 per month investment is already going towards future needs. Using a 10% annual compounding interest amount for the next 25 years, it could potentially grow to over $1.3 million. That's about $200,000 **less** than our projection. So, what would be the solution?

5. Either adjust the monthly savings amount **upward** (for example, from $1,000 to $1,250 with a potential growth of over $1.6 million) or reduce unnecessary future expenses (like that African Safari or beach house, or maybe just leave your 6 grandkids $5000 versus $10,000…don't tell them I suggested this!)

After pondering the details of this formula, however, here's the challenge that I already see regarding its validity: we don't have a *clue* when most of those expenses will be incurred, if ever! They most likely would be sprinkled over the entire 25 (graciously-given) years. If the cars need replacing in two years and the renovations need to be done in five, how does one estimate the *total* future projected amount, when there is dipping into the pot along the way, steadily shrinking its value? One suggestion I can make as a layperson is to estimate long-range totals on the *high* end. Don't settle for the measly $1000 monthly investment, when you can push it to $1250 and beyond. And the more projected future expenses you can squeeze into your monthly household budget (e.g., future cars, travel and renovations), the less they'll need to be factored into the full scheme of things.

By the way, our projected 25-year need is high because we included a huge estimation of $1,000,000 for nursing home care alone. (Remember my Dad's costs? That was over ten years ago and he was in an ordinary Medicare-funded facility.) If correctly selected life insurance and long-term care policies are put in place, along with systematic saving, there would be less of a need to devote such an enormous chunk of our income towards investing for potential sickness blobs *now*. We could spend more of it on Mediterranean cruises, donating to inner-city ministries, or anything else our hearts desire!

The last 21 chapters have been littered with a great deal of calculative cuisine. (And I'm sure much of it has been hard to swallow!) Life always seems to hurl the "w-h" questions towards us, doesn't it? Who, what, when, where, and how? How do we make dollars-and-cents decisions today in preparation for tomorrow? What measuring stick will help us determine the right amount needed for the future? When do we need to stop piling up snowflakes on the slope? Where do I turn for investment advice? Who can I trust to give me the kind of guidance that will secure the coverage of my future living *and* sick-care needs? When I can't make my own financial decisions, who will make them for me? And if I've done a good job of curbing my spending and snow-balling my savings, how do I decide who gets the snowball when I die? Dear reader, I *too* am still seeking answers to some of these questions.

As you would agree, the goal of predicting the future based upon the present can hardly be set in stone. All of our days are numbered by the Lord (Job 14:5), and even if we knew how many there were, we still wouldn't know what life circumstances will be encountered from the womb to the tomb, much less, how much those circumstances will cost us. The real issue is not found in answering questions such as *where can I find the best financial advisor or insurance agent,* or *what percentage of income should I save*? While writing this book, I uncovered a shocking oxymoron.

> Financial planning for a secure future is a farce, because no man can predict the future.

If the truth were told, the term, *financial planning* for a secure future is a farce, because **no man can predict the future**. It really boils down to how you view money and its purpose. By you reading this book, it's evident that you've been given a certain degree of intelligence. If you were to take that God-given intelligence and allow it to be shaped into a philosophy of stewardship, many of your money woes will vanish. This is the bottom line: you have been given a certain amount of income and assets. How hard and how long you work affects those two entities. It is your job to be the best steward that you can be, and not squander your best wealth-building asset like the Prodigal Son in the Bible (Luke 15: 11-32), ending up with nothing to show for it. If you establish an honest work ethic, curb frivolous spending, and make the most use of your income without taking undue risk, you'll be amazed at what you can accomplish. And whatever you do, don't use the Joneses as a standard of measure! They're stuck in the mud and quite comfortable being there!

· TWENTY-TWO ·

The Audit

Congratulations! You have achieved what the Joneses refuse to address: preparation for the future. How does it feel to expose the holes of debt, bury the corpses of credit, and breathe life into your budget? Your financial future has been raised from the dead! Your voyage is now *fantastic*! You have plunged head-first into the stream of financial demise, determined to locate the one thing that's been clotting your progress. You have dissolved the sickening spending habits, restoring your finances to good health.

You began by holding your entire portfolio in the palm of your hand, didn't you? Mere pennies captured beneath the sofa's cushions. Perhaps a dollar or two that began to mount each time you chose water over the Friday night fruity drink. Then your snowball became too heavy to hold, so you dumped it into a financial "wheelbarrow" and rolled it into an investment. It began to take shape as you pushed it along, causing it to get bigger and bigger, until you needed help moving it. You selected a reputable financial advisor to manage your precipitous product and arranged for automatic bank transfers to self-propel the growth. Thanks to consistent investing, compounding interest, and time, your snowball is now rolling with only a fraction of effort from yourself. Your finances have gone from the red to the black. Whee!

But hold up! The books may not all be balanced. There may be one last red entry on the docket. One overlooked debt. In fact, it's the ultimate debt that drives all of our wants and needs; and we just can't seem to shake it off. It's another alien from another world.

Another Alien Invasion
We had it all. More riches than the richest billionaire on earth. Everything we could have imagined and then some. It was ours for the asking. Better yet, we didn't even have to ask. It was destined to always be at our disposal. What happened to our riches? What happened to our abundance? What happened to our perpetual supply of health, wealth, and happiness? What caused our fortunes to vanish in less than a nanosecond? The culprit is none other than the master alien…the daddy of all debt…the blob from **within**.

"I thought we froze the blob," you might insist. *"I thought we hurled it into outer space, back to its destructive world, vowing never to allow it to attach itself to our lives again. How and when did it return?"* My friend, this is a *new* blob, a new alien, a *new* villain that vows *never* to release its deadly tentacles of indebtedness in this

world and beyond. This blob is imprinted in our ledger and cannot be erased by us. It cannot be wielded on a stick or frozen and carted off. This blob isn't made of physical matter. My friend, this blob is *spiritual*.

The Great Collapse

Millions lost millions during The Great Depression. Banks closed, soup lines opened, and businessmen jumped to their deaths in a state of utter despair and hopelessness. Even the great Caldwell & Company, the largest financial holding company in the South, collapsed under the weight of economic uncertainty.[39]

> This blob is imprinted in our ledger and cannot be erased by us.

That's also what happened in *our* banks, *our* corporations, if you will. Didn't know you owned one? We all do! In fact, we *are* a corporation! We are the CEO, teller, and auditor, all rolled into one. We run things, perform checks and balances, and take inventory of our affairs, assessing how we measure up to our own standards. We're even our own janitor, cleaning up obvious "spills" in our lives, and sometimes sweeping minor messes under the rug. That's what happens in each of our individual banks; namely, *The First National Bank of Me*.

When did this great collapse begin? you might ask. Long before our births, somewhere between the creation of Earth and the creation of mankind. In the Bible, chapters 1 and 2 in Genesis unfold the beginning of time (as we measure time) when God created the heavens, earth, angels, animal kingdom, vegetation, and ultimately, mankind (consisting of man and woman.) Man was different from the rest of Creation. God assembled a unique blend of dirt, shaped it into the form of a man, and breathed physical life into it. Because God is Spirit, His breath also gave spiritual life. Thus, man became a physical *and* spiritual being.

God named the man Adam, and Adam immediately went to work. He was productive, not because he had a debt to pay, but a God to please. He was a perfect man made in God's image, and their relationship was perfect. God ruled and Adam willingly submitted. Adam enjoyed the privilege of worshipping God.

Knowing that none of the animals was a suitable companion for Adam, God gave him the *only* suitable partner, a woman, a wife, who was named Eve by her husband. Theirs was a perfect union as well. Adam not only had a life of luxury, he knew his God-given responsibilities and was well equipped to fulfill them: reproduce, rule the Creation, and rest in God's provisions. Work was pleasant, food was plentiful, and his wife was spectacular! In all likelihood, life for all eternity would be smooth-sailing, steered by an all-loving God, the CEO of Man.

The Bank Hold-Up

Chapter 3 of Genesis recounts a series of events that marred God's perfect creation. The first couple on earth knew the enormity of their God-ordained freedom. They knew that He had provided a smorgasbord of tastefully delicious morsels from which they could feast. The only caveat to their meal choices was one tree, the tree of knowledge of good and evil. The caveat came with a clearly expressed consequence: *you eat, you die.*

One day a new player in town approached the bank, hoping to make a withdrawal: the devil, the master marketeer of debt. Created a perfect angel, Satan (once called Lucifer) formerly led the angels in praise and worship of God. He was beautiful, blameless, and always at the beck and call of his Creator. His allegiance to God was unwavering and unrestrained…until an audit revealed his deficiency, and he was declared bankrupt (Ezekiel 28:13-15). What drained his account? A blob. Not the kind on a stick, but a blob from within; the blob of "wants": wanting to rule; wanting to make his own choices; wanting to be "number one" and get the glory. He wanted to be CEO of the universe; simply, he wanted to be God. The blob from within was blatant rebellion against Almighty God, and it was an inexcusable sin.

> The blob from within was blatant rebellion against Almighty God, and it was an inexcusable sin.

In our lives, when we experience a financial fiasco, we have the option of declaring Chapter 7 or Chapter 13 bankruptcy. Chapter 13 allows us to work through our financial dilemma until it is repaid.[40] But unlike us humans, Satan was not given the option of facing his Debtor and drafting a repayment plan. His debt was exposed, he was condemned and sentenced to everlasting punishment, and he and his followers (other rebellious angels) were immediately evicted from heaven. Their landing pad was earth and their angelic state became that of a demonic nature. And so, it was in the Garden of Eden that Satan came looking to market his disease of defiance in hopes that it would go viral.

From Riches to Rags

Satan had one agenda: cast doubt on the goodness of God and stir up dissatisfaction, which would ultimately lead to rebellion. He wanted Man to be as bankrupt as he was. His approach was calculating and captivating. He repeated on earth what he began in heaven, trying to usurp authority; only this time it was over man, the one made in the image of God. So, Satan embodied a serpent and marched right past the husband, usurping his God-ordained authority in the family, and engaged in a direct marketing scheme with his wife. No billboards. No 30-second commercials. Just a simple question of doubt: "DID GOD SAY…"

Let's read the dialogue:

> [1]*Now the serpent was more cunning than any beast of the field which the LORD God had made. And he said to the woman, "Has God indeed said, 'You shall not eat of every tree of the garden'?"* [2] *And the woman said to the serpent, "We may eat the fruit of the trees of the garden;* [3] *but of the fruit of the tree which is in the midst of the garden, God has said, 'You shall not eat it, nor shall you touch it, lest you die.'"* [4] *Then the serpent said to the woman, "You will not surely die.* [5] *For God knows that in the day you eat of it your eyes will be opened, and you will be like God, knowing good and evil"* (Genesis 3:1-5 NKJV).

Satan's question was subtle. Eve's response was inaccurate. Satan's rebuttal was inviting. What happened next? I've penned the scene in a short poem:

More
When God's gracious gifts towards man were outpoured,
He gave in abundance for all to enjoy,
Especially the gift of Himself, to adore,
But our hearts were set on a little bit more.

Let's continue in verses 6-7:

> [6]*So when the woman saw that the tree was good for food, that it was pleasant to the eyes, and a tree desirable to make one wise, she took of its fruit and ate. She also gave to her husband with her, and he ate.* [7]*Then the eyes of both of them were opened, and they knew that they were naked; and they sewed fig leaves together and made themselves loin coverings* (NKJV).

The Great Break
One word... One glance... One bite, and Adam and Eve took their eyes off the true Treasure. Their source of satisfaction. Their source of security. Their source of life itself.

Adam and Eve had all that they needed. All they had to do was *not* do, *not* eat one piece of fruit. **But in that moment, that life-altering moment, when their teeth broke the skin of the forbidden fruit, they broke a perfect world, unleashing an unending flow of forbidden juices: the juices of pride, position, and pleasure.**

The blob of rebellion attached itself to their hearts, and they began filling their sacks with the wrong things, starting with a vain cover-up of their sin. The vault, once overflowing with God's riches, was raided. All of its treasures were looted, and The First National Bank of Me, a shell of a building, was left standing without spiritual life and void of all riches.

An Unexpected Birth

They were dead. Adam and Eve were dead. Yes, they wiped the luscious juice from their lips, but they were dead. Their dilated pupils saw their nakedness, but they were dead. They completed a crash course in sewing, but they were dead. The fig leaves provided a physical covering, but their offense was more than physical; it was spiritual. And the spiritual covering from the Great "I AM" (Exodus 3:14) had been removed and could not be restored by the hands of man; not then and not ever. **They had given birth to death**. The countdown towards physical death was ticking away moment-by-moment, but the devastation of spiritual death, separation from God, was **instantaneously** realized.

Life Without God

For the first time, Adam and his wife were alienated from God and stripped of everything of value. The big bank heist had happened. Their "crime" of needing and wanting *just a little bit more* cost them everything. They fell, and they fell **far**:

- From light to darkness
- From sight to blindness
- From life to death
- From innocence to guilt
- From unity to enmity
- From blessed to bankrupt

There they were, the first couple, dead in their sins and left to fend for themselves in the flesh, their condemned, corrupted flesh. In their own strength, they tried to work out the mess, or at least the *evidence* of it. In their pursuit to gain "all knowledge," they had violated God's command and they were toast. What a mess. What a muddy mess. What a monumental, muddy mess.

The If Onlys

If only they had been satisfied with God. If only they had loved Him and believed Him with all of their hearts. If only they had trusted in His provision. If only they had been submissive to His ways and His will. If only they had savored the joy and privilege of being God's greatest creation, rather than wanting to be self-proclaimed *know-it-alls*. If only they had relished their rich relationship with the One True God. If only they had believed His words to be true.

If only is costly, and it *only* gets worse…

Verses 8-13:

> *⁸ They heard the sound of the LORD God walking in the garden in the cool of the day, and the man and his wife hid themselves from the presence of the LORD God among the trees of the garden. ⁹Then the LORD God called to the man, and said to him, "Where are you?" ¹⁰ He said, "I heard the sound of You in the garden, and I was afraid because I was naked; so I hid myself." ¹¹ And He said, "Who told you that you were naked? Have you eaten from the tree of which I commanded you not to eat?" ¹² The man said, "The woman whom You gave to be with me, she gave me from the tree, and I ate." ¹³ Then the LORD God said to the woman, "What is this you have done?" And the woman said, "The serpent deceived me, and I ate"* (NKJV).

God had come in His usual manner, to fellowship with the husband and wife, but this time would be different. Shame was in the air, and its stench could not be dispelled. Despite the couple's feeble attempt to cover their mess, it was useless. God was coming, and He was coming with questions. The day of reckoning was upon them. The Auditor had arrived and would be taking inventory. There were no funds in the vault, the account fell short of perfection, and the books could not be reconciled. The human CEOs resorted to making excuses for their self-imposed deficiencies. The buck was passed (no pun intended) and the parties were pronounced guilty as charged.

"What Have You Done?"
Pardon me while I fast forward to the 21st Century. The people are different, but the question remains the same: "Sir, Madam, what have you done?" Take your rightful place in the Garden. You and your spouse had it all. The perfect Maker. The perfect marriage. The perfect reason for living: to love God in a perfect harmonious relationship. Every physical and spiritual closet bursting at the seams with the Lord's bounty, living a life attuned to His voice, His will, and His pleasure. Not a need to be needed. Not a want to be wanted.

Along comes a stranger pitching a different voice, proclaiming a different will, and proposing a different pleasure. In a moment's eye, the voice is accepted, the will is projected, and the pleasure is selected. Isn't it amazing how an itsy bitsy "need" can cause such eternal chaos in our lives? A need centered around the notion that, "I am independent, I can do whatever I want to do, and I will be accountable to no one for what I do?"

This book began with an admission of financial ruin, offering hope for the economic debacles in life. It insisted upon your need to "come clean" about all financial offenses before economic light could shine in a dark place. It outlined a blueprint for clearing away the mud and repaying all outstanding debts, from the least to the greatest, one payment at a time. Then it offered a plethora of ways to take the surplus and make it grow into a glorious financial reservoir for the future. You have handled all of your financial needs… Or have you?

The Needless "Needs"
We "need" so we get into all kinds of debt;
We "need" so we purpose to get out of debt;
We "need" so we save way beyond zero debt;
But spiritually speaking, our "need" is not met.

Adam and Eve's rebellion against God was the most devastating event in all of human history. It birthed a sinful nature, causing it to spread to all of us, **without exception**. Satan was successful. His suggestion of self-will infiltrated Man, and just as he had hoped, it *had* gone viral. Everything that's broken and wrong in this world, from our indebtedness to our ill-treatment of one another, is rooted in our self-centered wills and unrelenting desire to run our bankrupt banks.

> Adam and Eve's rebellion against God was the most devastating event in all of human history.

What's the Big Deal?
So, what's so sinful about sin? you may ask. **Everything**.

SIN

- has made us imperfect and unacceptable to God (Romans 3:23)
- has blinded us from the Truth of God's Way, Will, and Word (II Corinthians 4:4)
- has made us an enemy of God and placed us under His wrath (James 4:4; Romans 1:18)
- has condemned us **all** with the penalty of physical death (Hebrews 9:27)
- has sentenced us to eternal separation from God (spiritual death) and secured our reservation in hell (a literal place) after we die, forever and ever and ever… (II Thessalonians 1:5-9)
- has left us **without hope** (Ephesians 2:12)

Sin indwells us. It's not our second nature, it's our **sole** nature! It has invaded every aspect of our being: our minds, our wills, and our emotions. We *are* sin, we *do* sin, and we are *full* of sin. And this sin, this rebellion towards God, is our unpaid debt.

All of our efforts to pay off worldly debt are feeble, compared with our obligation to our *supreme* debt to the All-Supreme God. **We are born holding a weighty bag of debt towards God and He demands payment, on His terms.** Our good deeds won't outweigh it. Our giving won't outweigh it. Our so-called moral living won't outweigh it. Our sacraments, sacrifices, and self-inflicted sufferings won't outweigh it. Our chants, rites, and rituals won't outweigh it. Even our attempts to "pass the bag" to some imaginary reincarnated being will not remove the drain from each personal account. Just like Adam and Eve, we have no means of gaining the necessary resources within ourselves to pay it off; not a snowball's chance…

> We are born holding a weighty bag of debt towards God and He demands payment, on His terms.

What an ending. What an absolutely devastating ending. Having one's worldly finances in the black, but left with no peace, no purpose, and no position of right standing before the One and Only True God…

FREEZE! •

Are you in the red or black?

_____

_____

_____

· TWENTY-THREE ·

Order in the Court

There they were in a court of law; without a defense or way to vindicate themselves. They stood before the Judge, naked and unquestionably guilty as charged. The standard had been set: perfection. The law had been stated: *do not eat*. The punishment had been sanctioned: death (physically and spiritually).

Adam and Eve knew the death penalty had been imposed, and they were headed towards eternal punishment (Romans 6:23a). One final exhale of the very breath from God Himself, and they would transition from timed existence on Earth to timeless torture forever in hell, apart from His presence. God would not compromise His holy standards, not even for His beloved creation. If they could only find a way to pay their debt. They only needed one way… [41]

A Paradoxical Plan

It's true. God *would* accept payment, but it was no *Plan B* conjured up by man. It was an unbelievably paradoxical plan. Sin still had to be paid, but the *guilty* party's payment could only be paid by an innocent party. An innocent party had to die. An *innocent* party's blood had to be shed. The innocent had to be sacrificed for the guilty. This was the **only** way to appease God's fury and pay for the monumental sin of rebellion. And yet, Adam and Eve had no means to pay such a price, because goodness and righteousness had escaped them. So once again, they were toast. They were guilty, spiritually penniless, and standing right in the path of God's righteous judgment. But despite God's perfect law, even while His anger burned towards His rebellious creatures, His declaration of condemnation was overshadowed by the unimaginable. **God** paid the price.

More Than Skin

The debt of sin rested on the backs of Adam and Eve, yet their tainted flesh could not cover their rebellion towards the very One Who had given them life. Their human effort could never restore a relationship that was spiritual in nature. Their flawed efforts even trickled down to the physical, unraveling perfect unity among mankind. Whether physical or spiritual, there would be no harmony restored unless God stepped in.

> The LORD God made garments of skin for Adam and his wife, and clothed them.
>
> GENESIS 3:21 (NKJV)

And so, God went to work. Adam and Eve had missed seeing Him speak everything into existence during those six days mentioned in Genesis, but they were about to see a work like none other. Walk with me as we seek to peel back the workings of God's new work. *He made garments of skin…* We can only imagine how the events must have unfolded. To provide garments of skin for Adam and Eve, someone or *something* would have to lose theirs…someone or something would have to die. Adam and Eve were the only people on earth, so that left an animal as the only viable option…one with blood…one that would have to lose its life to pay for another…its innocent blood as a substitute for the guilty.

> In God's divine economy, the innocent had paid for the guilty, and man was once again reconciled to God.

Imagine the heartfelt sigh of relief and overwhelming sense of love when God brought the blood-stained garments to His recklessly defiant creatures, and covered every speck of their nakedness. With outstretched hands and unceasing tears, they joyously accepted His gift by faith, believing that it would satisfy their debt; thus, the price for their sin was paid in full.

But this act by God was more than mechanical. It was more than the transference of animal skin to human flesh. God had temporarily lost His treasure to the master called *sin*, and His people were enslaved with no hope of ever being freed. God's act of buying back mankind was saturated in His divine attribute of **love**; and from His love flowed grace and mercy. Two divinely polarized acts simultaneously at work. **Grace**: giving mankind what he did not deserve. **Mercy**: withholding what mankind *certainly* deserved. God, lawfully judging, but lovingly justifying. The touch of that warm skin against Adam and Eve's cold-hearted souls evidenced a work that God had never done before…a loving work of redemption. In God's divine economy, the innocent had paid for the guilty, and man was once again reconciled to God.

The Continuous Cover-Up

And so, they were restored. They were forgiven. They were vindicated from their crime of rebellion. Adam and Eve had had their sins covered by a gracious act of God, and once again, they had access to Him. Having had their accounts drained by unrighteousness, they were now granted a position of righteousness based upon His acceptance of the slain sacrifice. Although they would still face physical death (Genesis 3:22), their spiritual life, communion with God, had been reinstated.

That skin…that garment…that glorious cover-up extended to Adam and Eve. It was exactly what they had hoped for, but didn't know existed. But skins could only do so much. They could only **cover** sins, and cover *their* sins *alone*! What about their children's sins? What about their grandchildren's sins? Would mankind begin and end on their dime? Would Adam and Eve's error be a death blow for the entire human race? Well, yes and no.

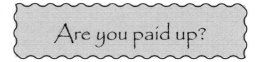

Are you paid up?

God, who is Eternal and all-knowing, was prepared for Man's rebellion before time existed. He knew that Adam and Eve would bankrupt the human race, and they and their descendants would need a way to reconcile their accounts in order to be restored to right standing and relationship with Him. So God made a promise; a promise not to cover sin in the future, but to take it away forever! A promise to take away its penalty, power, and presence. A promise to destroy the devil and all of his works. In fact, God promised to destroy death itself! And once again, God Himself would pay the price. He had the plan of redemption covered all along (Galatians 4:4-5)!

· TWENTY-FOUR ·

Riches on a Country Road

Early in my childhood when Dad decided to move us from a busy main thoroughfare to a quiet country setting, he selected a house that was situated in the middle of a large parcel of land and rested hundreds of feet from the main road. Technically speaking, we had neighbors, but most of them were too far away to see, much less, get to know.

Shortly after we moved in, my parents met the Coxes, an elderly black couple who lived a short distance down the road from our house. Next door to them was Mr. Cox's sister, Ethel, a spinster who was quite content with living by herself. They were the only other blacks living on our stretch of the road, so our families developed an instant bond. All of our other neighbors were white, but my Dad became acquainted with many of the husbands due to dealings in the community. Even in the 60's, there was mutual respect between the neighbors and my Dad, which I grew to appreciate later in life.

During the early years, Mom stayed at home, and she got to know a few of the wives as well. Her interactions were exclusively by telephone, since the distance prevented them from talking back and forth across boundary fences or yelling across a busy highway. Mom, too, was respected and liked by all who knew her. I witnessed the magnitude of this shortly after her death when one of the wives paid us a visit and while choking back tears, gently placed a homemade cake in my hands.

In the early 70's, Dad decided to have another home built closer to the road. We felt a little more like a part of a community, but the road was still a barrier to establishing real connections with the folks we had only come to know by name. The only time we kids crossed the road was to visit the Coxes with our parents, or as teenagers, to walk to the bus stop on days Dad didn't drop us off. Other than that, everyone stayed in their own neck of the woods.

Around the time that our home was being built, my cousin Alma came to live with us to attend the college where my parents worked. I have to admit, it took some adjustments to get used to having another *female* share my space, but I quickly grew to love her as the sister I never had. Despite the six-year difference in our ages, we managed to do a lot of things together, and life was filled with fun, laughter, and adventure. Her light-hearted personality brought an added joy to the Peoples household.

Faces Across the Road

One day, we noticed a young white couple getting out of their car parked in the driveway of the house directly across the road from us. They had apparently purchased the quaint little one-story brick home and moved in without us noticing. The large oak tree situated in the front yard shaded their porch from the scorching hot Virginia sun. The position between our front porch and their straight and narrow driveway was almost a perfect beeline. During the times when my family and the couple managed to arrive at or leave home around the same time, we would all throw up our hands and wave. Courtesy was always expressed in the country, no matter the color of one's skin. As time went on, Alma and I began to look for any signs of the couple's presence when we went in or out of our house, or when we relaxed on the front porch.

Spring and summer afternoons were usually spent hanging out on our front porch, swatting at passing bumble bees and admiring floating butterflies. It felt good just to be able to enjoy the country sights and sounds: car after car passing; truck after truck passing; a nearby tractor plowing up the black earth. That was pretty much the extent of our sights, besides a stray dog or two. And they didn't scare us, thanks to our fearless German Shepherd, Butch!

"It's Time"

One uneventful afternoon while Alma and I reclined on the porch in our flimsy lounge chairs, she glanced across the road and pointed towards the brick house. She had noticed that the neighbors' car was home. Before I realized what was happening, we had abandoned our chairs and she was leading us across the front lawn, across the country road, and up the couple's driveway. Alma had insisted it was time to meet the neighbors.

A quick knock at the door, and we were warmly greeted by Jim and Gail Shelton, a pleasant young couple with no children. They invited us in and were overjoyed that we had decided to pay them a visit. We insisted that we had only come to say *hi*, but they extended our visit with small chat and refreshments. All it took was a move on our part and new friendships were formed. Their hospitality spurred us to wave every time we saw them in the yard, and to pay more unannounced visits.

Time went by, and we got to know Jim and Gail so well that when they had their first baby, they asked us to babysit. I was eager to oblige, until I discovered the particulars of the day in question. Alma had an evening college class, so there would be a 30-minute gap between the time the Shelton's left me with their tiny tot and Alma would arrive. Being a teenager who had never grown up around babies, that moment would prove to be the longest half-hour of my life! My heart leaped with joy the moment my Dad's headlights appeared in the driveway, dropping off Alma, knowing that help would soon be coming through the door! (I think Alma was exaggerating when she said she heard the baby crying from he driveway! True or not, I was grateful to hand over the little guy and his bottle to my well-experienced cousin!)

The Shelton's never seemed to be "put out" by our drop-ins. In fact, they seemed to welcome them. Each time we were in their presence, they seemed to emit a calm, sweet spirit. During our visits, they usually had the television on, which was fine with us. But their viewings were usually *religious* in nature. I was used to that too. After all, even as a youngster, who *didn't* watch the Billy Graham Crusades and wait for the infamous "Just as I Am" hymn to be sung? We had Bibles and Christian literature in our home, and often heard the words of Jesus. I was even curious about the red lettering within the Book but never bothered to inquire about it. I sometimes found myself peering up at the lighted picture of Jesus in our foyer, or flipping through the thin hardback book about the 12 Disciples, not having a clue of their significance. Yes, the things of the Lord were revered in my home, but not in my heart...

Church was the "call of duty" on Sunday, whether I understood what was going on or not! I filled in the answers on Sunday School worksheets and sang songs in the church hymnal, but the things of God were no more interesting to me than ancient history. Our home was inundated with hymns sung by my parents at the spur of a moment. Dad's favorite was "Leaning on The Everlasting Arms," while Mom seemed to resound a Gospel warning through the lyrics of "Everybody Talkin' 'bout Heaven Ain't Goin' There." So, in the presence of the Shelton's, I was courteous towards their religious rhetoric, but it didn't stir me...until it stirred me...

A Tug After the Meal

One day, Alma and I received an invitation to have dinner with the Shelton's, which we eagerly accepted. As evening approached, we dressed comfortably but quickly, pounced out the front door and across the lawn, and cautiously skipped across the busy road and up the straight and narrow driveway like many times before. Jim greeted us at the door and ushered us into the den, with which we had grown accustomed. Small talk commenced while Gail added the finishing touches to her carefully planned meal. One by one, she garnished the table with an entrée, veggies, bread, drink and dessert. Her perfectly round beef patties were topped with a fruity ring of some sort. What a beautifully prepared meal for young ladies who were mere strangers to them just a few months beforehand. We bowed our heads as always, and Jim offered a prayer of thanksgiving for the food. Gail even clasped her baby's extended fingers together as prayer was offered. "Amen" was spoken in unison and we all dug in.

The subsequent events occurred almost seamlessly, so it's hard to recall how they all unfolded. Dinner ended, and Gail began to clear the table while the rest of us made our way to the den; that quaint little room that always had a subtle peace about it. Or was the peace radiating from this couple? It was hard to tell. Jim sat to our left while Gail soon joined us and chose the oversized chair to our right.

She reached towards the end table and took hold of her green Living Bible, the one from which s.
always read, while we sat politely and reverently, not daring to interrupt the recitations.

A few sentences into the reading and I began to sense a change, not in the setting, but in the words, and
even within myself. This time, the talk in the den was not light chatter. This time it was seriously searing,
and an uneasiness began to stir. Gail was speaking, but the essence of the words seemed to be radiating
from somewhere else. My feeling was indescribable at the time, but today I would label it as one of
nakedness. The covering of my soul was being peeled away, and I was grasping for cover; a leaf, a veil,
anything!

The Promise Revealed

A cover can *cover*, but it can never **take away** what's underneath it. Neither Adam, nor the rest of the
human race, was forgotten by God when the couple was expelled from the Garden of Eden. (Genesis
3:23-24). Animal sacrifices continued, generation after generation, in response to God's requirement,
each time temporarily covering the sins of the people; but they could never clear their guilty **consciences.**
The remembrance of sin was always before them (Isaiah 5:3; Psalm 51; Hebrews 9:14). And so, through
the ongoing ordeal of slaying innocent animals, the people hung on to that precious promise from God.
What was that promise, and when would it come? Certainly, it would be a permanent payment for
sin and declaration of man's innocence (Hebrews 9:12). The promise would bring permanent removal
of the wrath of God and restoration of man's righteousness (I Corinthians 1:30; Romans 5:9). It would
produce spiritual life and restored relationship with the God of the universe, with man one day residing
in a perfect physical body that would never die (II Corinthians 5:1). On top of that, God would seal His
promises with a Guarantee (Ephesians 1:13-14). God's Promise was a perfect human sacrifice. In fact, the
Promise was God **Himself**…He had arrived.

The Dynamic Duel

There He was, walking down that country road. Lingering
footprints lay undisturbed in the dust as he headed straight
towards my soul. The promised Sacrifice (John 1:29). He said
He would come, but I hadn't heeded the call. Light was being
shone on the dark reality of my bankruptcy and barrenness,
and I was rejecting it. The words spoken were plain: *God was
Holy, yet loved me.* The words spoken were piercing: *I was
in desperate need of a Savior.* The words spoken were pulling
me towards Him and away from my leaf, my veil, my every
excuse for not acknowledging Him as the only way to eternal
life. There He was, ready to embrace and forgive…and I was
pushing Him away.

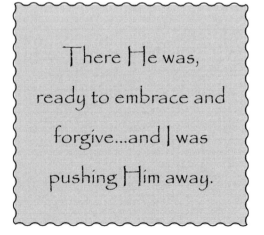

There He was, ready to embrace and forgive…and I was pushing Him away.

ᴛe Showdown

ᴛhe showdown was real. The war that began in heaven, shifted to Earth, and intensified in the Garden was coming to a climax. The enmity surged between two seeds spoken of in Genesis 3:15, and they were going toe-to-toe! It would be a fight to the finish...

One seed was Satan's and his demonic followers, who would lock horns with God over the souls of men. The other seed, the seed of the woman, was none other than God Himself, in the Person of Jesus Christ (Galatians 3:16). The bruising of his **heel** signified the death of Jesus Christ on the Cross (Acts 2:23). The bruising of his **head** signified the final crushing blow from God when the works of the devil would be destroyed (Romans 16:20).

> "And I will put enmity between thee and the woman, and between thy seed and her seed; it shall bruise thy head, and thou shalt bruise his heel."
>
> GENESIS 3:15 (NKJV)

God, the *Promise*? No doubt! *God*, coming to *Earth*? In the flesh (John 1:14). *God*, the *sacrifice*? Without question. *God would die*? He had to! Otherwise there would be no defeat (Hebrews 9:24-28). The catastrophic mess in the Garden that marred the image of God's glory and majesty would one day be undone. Death, guilt, and shame were buried deep within the recesses of the human soul through Adam's disobedience, and they had to be unearthed and eradicated. And that same excavation needed to begin in my very own heart...

The Bank Takeover

And so, the righteous coup began. Through the voice of my newfound neighbor, the truth of God's Words had been spoken and the seriousness of the crime had been exposed. My righteousness had been audited and declared bankrupt, with no possible means of working off the debt. I needed a Savior to rescue me from the penalty of sin. I needed a Redeemer to pay my debt in full. I needed a Judge to declare me righteous. I needed to tear down The First National Bank of Me and receive the Lord as the CEO of a new structure. I needed to be born again.

It was time for a decision and I bowed my head to repeat in my heart what was being prayed out loud. Jim prayed words of God's love, which I acknowledged. Words of God's holiness and righteousness, which I acknowledged. Words about Jesus, God in the flesh, as the Only One qualified to die for the sins of man, which I acknowledged. Words of my guilt...**uh oh**!

Once again, I found my fingertips reaching for that crumbling leaf, that worthless covering used to shield my total depravity. Like Adam and Eve, I fought to point fingers in any direction possible, struggling to detract from the emptiness in my vault, the guilty stain in my ledger, the certainty of my imperfection. In my unworthiness, I sought to hide my nakedness before the Almighty God, searching under every religious "bush" in a desperate attempt to uncover any shred of innocence on my part. But none existed. None could be found. Even while I crouched behind a fig leaf of failure and doom, it took the mighty hand of a loving God to drag me from behind my self-righteousness, kicking and screaming, and convict me of *me*! It was at that point that I bowed in submission to receive Jesus Christ as my personal Lord and Savior.

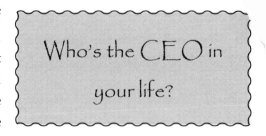

Riches Restored

A new bank with a new Owner had been erected! I knew I was saved. I knew I was forgiven. I knew I had a relationship with God. I had skipped across that country road hours before, lost and condemned to eternal punishment. I strolled back in the moments before sunset, glancing up at the picturesque sky and faintly whispering, *God*… Yes, my account was not only full, but all debts were paid in full! The riches of life snatched by the evil one had been deposited back into my account, and I was free of all crimes, **past, present, and future**! The vault stood overflowing with treasures I never knew existed. And over 40 years later, they continue to grow exponentially!

· TWENTY-FIVE ·

A New Audit

There are two sets of books that clearly reveal the state of my holdings. The first is housed at various financial institutions, revealing the worth of my **temporal** riches. Past and present ledgers show my progression from full-fledged indebtedness to less indebtedness to a debt-free state. They show a shift from *ridiculously red-hot* years in arrears to a relentless tenacity to bust the blob of debt. They show the accumulation of financial snowflakes and the rate at which other flakes were added. They reveal the ups and downs of the economic market and my weathering of the storm, resulting in steady financial risings. They show a determination to stay in the *black*, build a sizeable nest egg, and prepare for the potentially costly health challenges in the future, while helping needy brothers and sisters along the way. They show a pattern of life of someone endeavoring to use the funds entrusted to her by the Lord in a manner that displays good stewardship, and that will bring honor and glory to His name. In essence, they show hard and tedious work that will hopefully pay well in the end.

There's another book that reveals the state of my **spiritual** holdings, but the work done to amass the wealth contained in it wasn't done by me! In fact, **any** work on my part would have been disallowed as an entry. This Book is the Book of Life (Revelation 3:5; 21:27). This Book was written before the foundation of the world and contains every name of every person who will enter eternity in right standing before God, with all accounts reconciled (Revelation 13:8). This Book contains the beneficiaries of that precious promise, the promise that was fulfilled in Jesus Christ.

The Perfect Promise

The layers of the promise unfold like a fragrant rose, releasing more and more of its magnificent aroma with each exposed petal:

- Jesus veiled His Divine Nature, and allowed Himself to be born of a virgin. (A perfect birth - Isaiah 7:14; Philippians 2:5-8).
- He lived on Earth without committing one sin. (A perfect life - Hebrews 4:15).
- He willingly offered Himself as a sacrifice for the sins of man. (A perfect submission - Hebrews 9:28).
- Jesus died on a Cross built for the guilty, but borne by the Innocent. (A perfect sacrifice -II Corinthians 5:21).

- Jesus' death appeased the wrath of the Father and satisfied the payment for sin. (A perfect payment - Romans 3:24-25).
- His death removed the enmity between man and God, restoring harmony once for all. (A perfect relationship - Romans 5:1,10).
- Jesus' resurrection in His physical body guaranteed resurrected and incorruptible bodies for His born-again children. (A perfect transformation - I Corinthians 15:51-54).
- Jesus' resurrection snatched the devil's power of death, replacing it with eternal life. (A perfect destruction - Hebrews 2:14).

The Finished Work

Yes, Jesus was at work before time began. He was at work when He kicked the Deceiver and his bandits out of heaven. He was at work when He covered the sins of His first rebellious couple. He was at work when He allowed the Holy Spirit to overshadow Him in the womb of a virgin and was born in a manger (Luke 2:12). He was at work when he blessed naysayers and self-righteous folks, while pouring His life into 12 contrary men, one of whom would betray Him in the end (John 6:71; Luke 22:4).

Jesus was still at work when they arrested Him and falsely accused Him, and beat Him to an unrecognizable state (Luke 22:63-64). He was at work when those closest to Him denied Him at the most crucial hour (Matthew 26:71-72). He was at work when they stripped Him of His clothing and mocked His authority (Mark 15:20). He was at work when they forced Him to drag a cross for the guilty up Golgotha Hill (John 19:17). He was at work when they severed the most sensitive nerves in His hands and feet with the tips of rusty jagged nails (Acts 2:23).

Jesus kept on working when they nailed the sign, *Jesus of Nazareth, the King of the Jews,* over His blood-stained brow (John 19:19) and He cried, *Father, why have You forsaken Me* (Matthew 27:46)? He was at work when He took His last breath and died (Matthew 27:50). And three days later (*Hallelujah*), He was at work when He arose from the grave in bodily form in all of His glory, snatching the keys of death and hell from the devil (Luke 24:46; I Corinthians 15:3-4; Revelation 1:18).

Jesus ascended back to His home, heaven. He is forever making intercession on behalf of His redeemed children (Hebrews 7:25). We eagerly await His next promise…the promise to return to Earth, transform our corruptible physical bodies into incorruptible bodies, and remove us from the very presence of sin **forever** (I Corinthians 15:51-57).

The Invitation

Those whose names are in the Book of Life have a standing invitation to dine with the Savior of the world one day in heaven (Revelation 19:9). Will you be present? Will you be seated at the table and partake of the meal especially prepared by the Lord? Will you be clothed in a spotless garment, not made from

...ruptible animal skin, but a righteous garment? Will you be clothed ...a the righteousness of Christ?

In heaven there are no IOU's. No debt-busting worksheets. No laboring to pay an eternal debt with temporal means. No bloody animal sacrifices. The Lamb of God has come. Spurred by His matchless love, He came to this sinfully sick world, lived among the vilest of the vile, healed the sick and raised the dead, while the whole time, wooing Man to come to Him… come to Him…come to Him…

In heaven there are no IOU's.

To come is to confess (Romans 10:9). To come is to believe (John 1:12-13). To come is to trust and receive, by faith, the unsearchable riches of God's grace: Jesus Christ, the Gift of forgiveness, reconciliation, and regeneration.

I found my riches on a country road. Will you find yours? Why don't you come? His work is settled in heaven.

It is finished…

APPENDIX A: Pat's Million-Dollar Money Wasters

WASTERS	ORIGINAL DATE	ENDING DATE	MONTHLY (or lump sum) WASTE	NO. OF WASTED PAYOUT YEARS (+uninvestable years)	PROJECTED EARNINGS (compounded annually at 10%)	POTENTIAL EARNINGS INVESTED with & without additional monthly contributions
Failure to save $100 per month per Benefits Director	10/1983	10/2011	$100	28 years	$184,584	$184,584
Money from paid off car and house (uninvested)	06/2003	6/2011	$800	8 years	$117,919	$117,919
Income forfeited from working only 4 days a week	10/1990	10/1999 10/2011	$800	9 years +12 years	$140,403 Lump sum invested 12 yrs.	$463,842
Stock Trading	05/2005	05/2011	$12K (LS)	6 years	$21,811	$21,811
Variable Annuity	09/1998	09/2006 09/2011	$500	8 years + 5 years	$73,700 Lump sum invested 5 yrs.	$122,259
Real Estate Investing	04/2003	04/2011	$12K (LS)	8 years	$26,618	$26,618
Income Overpayment	09/2007	09/2011	$29,000	4 years	$43,191	$43,191
Whole Life Insurance	09/1977	09/1985 09/2011	$50	8 years +26 years	$7,370 Lump sum invested 26 yrs.	$98,165
House Note & Utilities at *The Grave McMansion*	10/2010	10/2011	$1,300	1 year	$16,471	$16,471
Down Payment & Moving Expenses	10/2010	10/2011	$12K (LS)	1 year	$13,257	$13,257

Total Money Wasted Up to 2011   **$1,108,117**

APPENDIX B: **Snowball Investing Budget Form**©

Income

Paycheck (after taxes)..$ _____

Extra Income..$ _____

Total Income ....$ _____

Giving ....$ _____

House Expenses

Mortgage / Rent ....$ _____

Mortgage / Renter's Insurance.........................$ _____

Utilities ....$ _____

Internet, Cable, Phones ....$ _____

Maintenance ....$ _____

Other House Expenses.......................................$ _____

Other..$ _____

Food

Groceries ....$ _____

Lunch ....$ _____

Eating Out ....$ _____

Transportation

Gas ....$ _____

Car Loan...$ _____

Car Insurance ....$ _____

Car Maintenance...$ _____

Car Repairs ....$ _____

Parking / Tolls ....$ _____

Bus / Transit Costs ....$ _____

Other..$ _____

Total for Column One....................................$ _____
(Excluding Income)

Health

Health Insurance...$ _____

Life Insurance ....$ _____

Other Insurance ....$ _____

Medicine & Medical Supplies...........................$ _____

Other Routine Expenses ....$ _____

Family / Personal Expenses

Laundry/Dry Cleaning ....$ _____

Child Care ....$ _____

Alimony/Child Support....................................$ _____

Clothing/Accessories..$ _____

Extracurricular/Sports Clubs ....$ _____

Entertainment...$ _____

Other..$ _____

Education

Private Education ....$ _____

Tutoring ....$ _____

School Supplies ....$ _____

Finance / Debts

911 Savings ....$ _____

Unexpected Expense Savings ....$ _____

Investments...$ _____

Bank Account Fees..$ _____

Credit Card Debt...$ _____

School Debt ....$ _____

Personal Debt ....$ _____

Other Debt ....$ _____

Total for Column Two....................................$ _____

INCOME...$ _____

Minus EXPENSES ....$ _____

Excess or Deficit..$ _____

*This form may be photocopied for personal use
without prior permission from the Author.*

APPENDIX C - 1 EXAMPLE:
Example of Snowball Investing Muddy Mess Form©

Start Date 01/01/2018

(10% of each balance is being added to equal the *Real Debt*.)

Creditor	Current Balance	Interest Rate	Real Debt	Late Fees	Monthly Payment	No. of Months Until Paid Off	MUD FREE DATE
Overpriced Electronics	$1200	10%	$1320	$25	$100	13	01/19
ABC Visa Card	$2500	10%	$2750	$25	$50	55	**02/23**
Private School Tuition	$20,000	10%	$22000	$25	$500	40	04/22

Use this example to complete your *Snowball Investing Muddy Mess©* form, listing all of your debts from smallest to largest amounts. In this example, 02/2023 would be the Mud Free Celebration Date when you become totally debt-free!

APPENDIX C - 2
Snowball Investing Muddy Mess Form©

Start Date _____ / _____ / _____

Creditor	Current Balance	Interest Rate	Real Debt	Late Fees	Monthly Payment	No. of Months Until Paid Off	MUD FREE DATE
	$	%	$	$	$		
	$	%	$	$	$		
	$	%	$	$	$		
	$	%	$	$	$		
	$	%	$	$	$		
	$	%	$	$	$		
	$	%	$	$	$		
	$	%	$	$	$		
	$	%	$	$	$		
	$	%	$	$	$		
	$	%	$	$	$		

This form may be photocopied for personal use without prior permission from the Author.

APPENDIX D
Snowball Accumulation Worksheet[©]

Categories	ANNUAL SAVINGS TOTAL
Beauty	$
Clothing and Accessories	$
Financials	$
House	$
Kids, Pets, and Pregnancy	$
Food	$
Utilities	$
Gardening and Landscaping	$
Car	$
Entertainment et al.	$
Gifts and Shopping	$
Technology and Electronics	$
Education	$
Sickness and Wellness	$
Travel	$
Miscellaneous	$
ANNUAL GRAND TOTAL	$
MONTHLY GRAND TOTAL (Annual Grand Total divided by 12)	$

This form may be photocopied for personal use without prior permission from the Author.
© 2018 Pat Peoples Smith

Example of:

Snowball Investing Category Running Balance Worksheet©

Month/Year: <u>12/2019</u>   **Category:** <u>Food</u>

Date	Transaction	Deposit or Withdrawal		Balance
11/30/19		$	($)	$150.00
12/01/19	Deposit from budgeted salary	$500.00	($)	$650.00
12/05/19	Groceries	$	($175.00)	$475.00
12/18/19	Desserts for potluck	$	($30.00)	$445.00
12/25/19	Holiday groceries	$	($ 200.00)	$245.00
12/31/19	Groceries	$	($145.00)	**$100.00**
12/31/19	**Transfer to Unexpected Expense Savings category**	$	**($100.00)**	$0
12/31/19	Deposit from budgeted salary (for January)	$500.00	($)	$500.00
01/01/20	Groceries	$	($100.00)	$400.00

At the end of each month, determine the amount of **surplus** funds that will be allocated towards debt, the 911 Savings, the Unexpected Expense Savings, and Investments. (In this example, the surplus was $100.) As each of the first three categories is fully funded, that amount allocated in your monthly budget can be transferred to the next savings area until you can snowball all three categories' allocations towards Investments!

APPENDIX E-2
Snowball Investing Category Running Balance Worksheet©

Month/Year: _____ / _____   Category: _____

Date	Transaction	Deposit or Withdrawal		Balance
__ / __ / __		$	($)	$
__ / __ / __		$	($)	$
__ / __ / __		$	($)	$
__ / __ / __		$	($)	$
__ / __ / __		$	($)	$
__ / __ / __		$	($)	$
__ / __ / __		$	($)	$
__ / __ / __		$	($)	$
__ / __ / __		$	($)	$
__ / __ / __		$	($)	$
__ / __ / __		$	($)	$
__ / __ / __		$	($)	$

APPENDIX F
Registered Trademarks and Public Figures

The Author and Apples of Gold Press recognize the following registered trademarks and public figures mentioned within the text:

AAA®, AARP®, Aigner®, Alfa Romero®, Amazon®, American Express®, Apple®, Blackberry®, Dave Ramsey®, Equifax®, Experian®, Facebook®, Forever Stamp®, General Motors (GM®), Google®, Happy Meal®, JCPenney®, Liquid Paper®, Lyft®, Monopoly®, Nasdaq®, Neiman Marcus®, 1964 New York World's Fair®, Oscar®, Pyrex®, Trans Union®, Turbo Tax®, Uber®, and Volvo®. Public figures include Larry Burkett (deceased), Clark Howard, and Dave Ramsey.

The Author acknowledges that the mention of these entities and public figures does not imply their affiliation with or endorsement, sponsorship, or support of this Author or the statements in this book.

· RESOURCES ·

Budget Worksheets

https://www.consumer.ftc.gov/articles/pdf-1020-make-budget-worksheet.pdf

www.crown.org

www.familylife.com

Investment Calculators

www.foundationsu.com/high-school

https://www.investor.gov/additional-resources/free-financial-planning-tools/compound-interest-calculator

Additional Financial and Stewardship Resources

Preparing for Retirement, by Larry Burkett. Moody Press, Chicago, IL 1992.

The Millionaire Next Door, by Thomas J. Stanley, Ph.D., and William D. Danko, Ph.D., Pocket Books, NY, 1996.

The Overload Syndrome: Learning To Live Within Your Limits, by Richard A. Swenson, M.D., NavPress, Colorado Springs, CO, 1998.

Margin: Restoring Emotional, Physical, Financial and Time Reserves to Overloaded Lives, by Richard A. Swenson, Colorado Springs, CO, 2004.

Pleasing People: How Not To Be An "Approval Junkie", by Lou Priolo, P & R Publishing, Phillipsburg, NJ, 2007.

Whose Money Is It Anyway?, by John MacArthur, Word Publishing, Nashville, TN, 2000.

· SOURCE NOTES ·

1   https://www.cnbc.com/2017/06/13/heres-how-many-americans-have-nothing-at-all-saved-for-retirement.html

Chapter 1

2   https://www.investordictionary.com/definition/rule-of-72

3   https://www.mylifesite.net/blog/post/so-ill-probably-need-long-term-care-but-for-how-long/

Chapter 2

4   https://en.wikipedia.org/wiki/There's_a_Hole_in_My_Bucket: Published: circa 1700

5   https://www.nerdwallet.com/blog/average-credit-card-debt-household

6   Priolo, Louis. *Pleasing People: How Not To Be an Approval Junkie*. Phillipsburg, NJ: P&R Publishing Company, 2007. Print.

7   https://www.marketwatch.com/story/most-americans-have-less-than-1000-in-savings-2015-10-06

8   https://en.wikipedia.org/wiki/The_Blob

9   https://www.thesimpledollar.com/heres-how-much-the-average-american-pays-in-interest-each-year/

Chapter 4

10   https://www.youtube.com/watch?v=n2FtlFFzyuw

11   https://www.azlyrics.com/lyrics/gloriagaynor/iwillsurvive.html

12   https://wallethub.com/edu/average-credit-card-interest-rate/50841/

Chapter 5

13   Bach, David. *Smart Couples Finish Rich*. New York: Broadway Books, 2001. Print.

Chapter 6

14   https://www.goodreads.com/quotes/4900-the-best-and-most-beautiful-things-in-the-world-cannot

15   https://www.npd.com/wps/portal/npd/us/news/press-releases/2018/us-prestige-beauty-industry-sales-rise-6-percent-in-2017-reports-the-npd-group/

16   (Hunter, J. & O'Donnell, K (Producers). Stilson, J. (Director). 2009. *Good Hair*. United States: Chris Rock Productions and HBO Films.)

Chapter 7

17   Kiyosaki, Robert., & Lechter, Sharon. *Rich Dad Poor Dad*. New York: Warner Books, 2002. Print.

Chapter 8

18   https://en.wikipedia.org/wiki/The_Money_Pit

Chapter 9

19   https://en.wikipedia.org/wiki/Yellow_pages

Chapter 10

20   https://www.swlondoner.co.uk/bigger-jesus-mcdonalds-golden-arches-recognisable-christian-cross

Chapter 14

21   https://www.hollywoodreporter.com/news/study-global-media-industry-poised-562694

22   https://www.fool.com/retirement/2018/10/18/you-wont-believe-how-many-americans-have-less-than.aspx

23   https://www.merriam-webster.com/dictionary/muse

24   Ad Sense Publishing Co., Chicago, Illinois: 1905 August, A Journal of Advertising and Business Building, Volume 19, Number 2, Advertising Definitions by W. T. O'Connor, Quote Page 121.

25   http://www.worldometers.info/world-population/

26   https://www.medicare.gov/Pubs/pdf/10116-Your-Medicare-Benefits.pdf

27   https://www.medicaidplanningassistance.org/medicaid-eligibility

28   https://www.medicaid.gov/medicaid/managed-care/guidance/index.html

Chapter 15

29   https://www.marketwatch.com/story/1-billion-in-gift-cards-go-unused-every-year-heres-how-to-avoid-that-2016-12-30

Chapter 17

30   https://www.daveramsey.com

Chapter 18

31   https://www.genworth.com/about-us/industry-expertise/cost-of-care.html

Chapter 20

32   http://www.women-inventors.com/Bette-Nesmith-Graham.asp

33   *The Millionaire Next Door*, Published 1996-10-25, Govt. Institution, authors Tomas. Stanley & William D. Danke.

Chapter 21

[34] https://en.wikipedia.org/wiki/Fantastic_Voyage

[35] http://www.storyarts.org/library/aesops/stories/tortoise.html

[36] Quote: Mark Selman, 10-25-18

[37] https://www.forbes.com/sites/financialfinesse/2017/11/20/how-much-money-is-really-enough/#6fd1d8766618

[38] https://www.moneycrashers.com/how-much-save-month-prioritize

Chapter 22

[39] https://www.federalreservehistory.org/essays/banking_panics_1930_31

[40] *Your Practical Guide for Saving, Spending and Investing,* by Chuck Bentley and Larry Burkett: Crown Financial Ministries, Inc., 2014, page 22.

Chapter 23

[41] https://www.gty.org/library/sermons-library/90-226/the-creation-of-man

· INDEX ·

· ABOUT THE AUTHOR ·

ALTHOUGH A NATIVE VIRGINIAN, PAT PEOPLES SMITH has branded herself as a Georgia Peach for over 35 years. She acknowledges having no financial credentials, but is uniquely qualified to pen her first book, *Snowball Investing*, on financial matters as a result of a family crisis and the knee-jerk urgency to transform her own finances while single. Using the principles of stewardship, she recounts in detail the steps taken to erase all debts and to create a comprehensive financial portfolio necessary to outweigh unforeseen future expenses.

Pat's first published work appeared in the book, *In Search of a Match Black & White*, by Dan Moore, Sr. She relives her journey with a perfect stranger, a leukemia patient in desperate need of a bone marrow or stem cell transplant. Their recollection of the donor/recipient process is highlighted from both vantage points. Over the last three decades, Pat has also penned an assortment of unpublished poems for personal encouragement.

Pat's college degrees in occupational therapy and counseling, as well as her past and present association with "helps" industries including real estate and the world-renown Reliv International, Inc., have given her a lifetime of opportunities to meet people in desperate and hurting places, and guide them towards a state of hope and purpose.

Pat can be contacted via her website, www.snowball-investing.com, and followed on her Facebook page, *Snowball Investing*. She shares practical money-saving tips and articles of inspiration to encourage readers to rid themselves of the debt "blob" in order to protect ones' greatest asset producer, their income. Pat enjoys reading, sewing, and travelling with her husband Sumner Anthony Smith. She is personally inspired each time she ministers at Gilgal, Inc., a faith-based drug and alcohol women's transitional facility in Atlanta. She is also active in her home church, Berean Bible Baptist Church in Atlanta.

Made in the USA
Columbia, SC
06 August 2019